Young Children and Picture Books
Literature From Infancy to Six

Mary Renck Jalongo

National Association for the Education of Young Children
Washington, D.C.

Mary Renck Jalongo is an early childhood educator, writer, reviewer, and editor. Her classroom
experience includes teaching toddlers, preschoolers,
first grade, and second grade. In 1983, Dr. Jalongo
was named Pennsylvania's Outstanding Young
Woman. Her articles have appeared in *Young Children, Childhood Education, The Reading Teacher,*
PTA Today, and as book chapters, and have won a national EDPRESS Award
for educational journalism and a Best Essay award from the Association for
Higher Education. As an editoral board member, Dr. Jalongo has worked with
NAEYC and ACEI. In 1988, she was named to Who's Who in U.S. Writers,
Editors, and Poets. Dr. Jalongo is also a consultant with Phi Delta Kappa
International. She received a B.A. from Mercy College of Detroit, an M.A.T.
from Oakland University, and a Ph.D. from the University of Toledo. Dr. Jalongo
is a professor at Indiana University of Pennsylvania where she teaches under-
graduate and graduate level courses in child development and the language arts.

Photo credits: © Skjold Photographers cover; Hildegard Adler 98, 102;
Esther Mugar 5; Subjects & Predicates 25; Steve Takatsuno 27; Michaelyn
Straub 28; Shulamit Gehlfuss 39; Jim Bradshaw 41; Michael Schulman 47;
Larry Pakyz 70; Marilyn Nolt 77; Jeffrey High 93.

National Association for the Education of Young Children
1509 16th St., N.W.
Washington, DC 20036–1426
202–232–8777 or 800–424–2460
Website:http://www.naeyc.org

Through its publications program the National Association for the Education
of Young Children (NAEYC) provides a forum for discussion of major issues
and ideas in the early childhood field, with the hope of provoking thought and
promoting professional growth. The views expressed or implied are not
necessarily those of the Association. NAEYC thanks the author, who donated
much time and effort to develop this book as a contribution to the profession.

Library of Congress Catalog Card Number: 88–62969
ISBN 0–935989–17–X
NAEYC #160

Design and production: Jack Zibulsky

Printed in the United States of America.

CONTENTS

Acknowledgments, vi

Preface, vii

Chapter One. The Importance of Children's Literature, 1
 A definition for literature, 5
 When is a book literature?, 6
 Attributes of literature, 6
 Learning through literature, 11
 What can children learn from literature?, 13
 Literature and the young child's developmental needs, 14

Chapter Two. What Is Quality Literature?, 17
 Formulating professional judgments about picture books, 18
 How difficult is it to write a children's book?, 20
 Deciding which books are good, 21
 Selecting books without racial, ethnic, or gender stereotypes, 24
 The child's perspective on quality, 26
 Books that children love, 33

Chapter Three. Bringing Picture Books and Young Children Together, 35
 Which book for which child, 43
 How to share a book with a young child, 49

Chapter Four. How Do Children Respond to Literature?, 57
 Influences on literary responses, 59
 How children learn to respond to literature, 59
 Observing young children's responses to literature, 62
 The child as critic, 66
 Sources of picture book appeal, 67
 Predicting how children will respond, 68
 Implications for practice, 68

Chapter Five. Parents, Children, and Picture Books, 73
 Reading aloud and learning to read, 74
 Is earlier necessarily better?, 76
 What children learn from listening to stories, 77
 How to share picture books with your child, 78

Chapter Six. The Teacher's Role in Promoting Picture Books, 87

Goals for the literature program, 90
A role description for teachers, 90
Teacher advocacy for literature, 93
The literature-based curriculum, 93
Theory into practice, 95
Picture books to build curriculum, 98

Conclusion, 111

Appendixes

A. Outstanding Picture Book Authors and Illustrators, 113
B. Picture Book Classics, 114
C. Picture Books That Celebrate Cultural Diversity and the Universality of Human Experience, 116
D. A Selected Bibliography of Picture Books on Videocassette, 118

ILLUSTRATIONS

Grandfather Twilight written and illustrated by Barbara Berger, 7

Bailey Goes Camping written and illustrated by Kevin Henkes, 9

The Patchwork Quilt by Valerie Flournoy, illustrated by Jerry Pinkney, 10

The Ugly Duckling retold by Marianna Mayer, illustrated by Thomas Locker, 19

Night in the Country by Cynthia Rylant, illustrated by Mary Szilagyi, 30–31

The Last Puppy written and illustrated by Frank Asch, 52–53

Ox Cart Man by Donald Hall, illustrated by Barbara Cooney, 58

Hazel's Amazing Mother written and illustrated by Rosemary Wells, 63

Mufaro's Beautiful Daughters: An African Tale written and illustrated by John Steptoe, 69

A Rhinoceros Wakes Me Up in the Morning by Peter Goodspeed, illustrated by Dennis Panek, 81

Just Us Women by Jeannette Caines, illustrated by Pat Cummings, 82–83

Fix-It written and illustrated by David McPhail, 84–85

"The Three Bears" from *Favorite Nursery Tales* written and illustrated by Tomie de Paola, 88

The Teddy Bears' Picnic by Jimmy Kennedy, illustrated by Alexandria Day, 89

The Biggest Pumpkin Ever by Steven Kroll, illustrated by Jeni Bassett, 104–105

ACKNOWLEDGMENTS

The words and drawings of young children give this book its vitality. Special recognition goes to the children's librarians of the Toledo-Lucas County Public Libraries and to the Early Childhood Education majors at Indiana University of Pennsylvania who interviewed children and gathered samples of children's work.

I am indebted to Marilyn Clark, Coordinator of Children's Services in the Toledo-Lucas County Public Libraries; Anne Creany, first grade teacher and doctoral advisee; and four preschool teachers, Frankie De George, Jamie Hodan, Sandy Malcom, and Sandy Monsilovich; for their cooperation and patience.

Finally, I would like to acknowledge a children's librarian who reviewed earlier drafts of this book and contributed to the book in the process, Melissa Renck. Last but not least, I would like to thank Denise Shaffer and Julie Hockinson for carefully proofreading and Michelle Yanoscsik for word processing the manuscript.

PREFACE

I am of the opinion that a book's table of contents should tell the reader what to expect, while the book's preface should alert the reader to the author's biases. Then, if readers choose to skip over the preface and disagree with the author, it will not be because the author failed to forewarn them.

Where children's literature is concerned, I am very opinionated. The picture book is much more than something to do during story-time. It is the basis for becoming a literate adult, one who not only decodes words accurately but also *enjoys* reading and *makes* the time to read. Research has recently validated this fact, which the Progressive Educators explored and brought into the nation's better nursery schools, day care centers, kindergartens, and primary grades during the first half of the 20th century. Early childhood educators who enthusiastically share quality picture books with young children are promoting literacy in the fullest sense of the word. Knowing this, expert early childhood teachers have always made high-quality children's picture books a central part of their curriculum. Ideally, a child first learns to love books during infancy. Despite the importance of early experiences with literature, many young children arrive at schools and centers lacking experience with picture books. For them especially, and for all the other children in our care, we have an obligation to bring children and books together.

In order to realize the full potential of children's literature, adults must accept at least three basic precepts: that the overriding purpose of picture books is enjoyment, that children's literature is a legitimate subject for adult study, and that children can learn as much from fiction as they can from fact.

Begin With Enjoyment

Although children certainly do learn from picture books, the process must begin with enjoyment rather than as a lesson. Pleasure persuades the child first to look, then to discuss and listen, next to remember, and finally to read a favorite story. Enjoyment is the force that sustains a young child's involvement with picture books when toys and television beckon. The enjoyment of picture books is a precursor of adult literacy and literary appreciation.

The Picture Book Is an Art Form

A second common misconception is that children's literature is really "kiddie lit" — cute little books that are unworthy of serious consideration by adults. The reading level and content are simple, so one book seems as good as another. The truth, of course, is that even the simplest concepts can be presented in a superb, mediocre, or inferior way. Furthermore, children's literature is not only worthy of being read to children by adults, it is also the subject of theory and research, of literary and artistic criticism, and of social controversy.

Fact Is No Better Than Fantasy

A third misconception about children's literature has to do with fantasy and humor. Picture books without an obvious lesson or moral are often viewed even less favorably by adults. "What if children really try to do some of the ridiculous things in this story?" "Won't a child be confused by things that couldn't happen in real life?" "What are they really *learning* from this book?" I use these questions as examples because they are remarks that I hear (or overhear) each time I teach a children's literature course. It is fascinating that so many adults impose these limitations on children's literature without placing similar restrictions on their own reading choices. The same adults who stop reading a book because they "can't get into it" often think that children's books should be like a children's vitamin supplement—a daily dosage with a sweet, colorful outer shell. Imagination, spontaneity, insight—abilities like these require as much cultivation as knowledge and skills. Picture books are a primary source of stimulation for creative thinking processes.

The best way to communicate these ideas is to give adults experience in bringing quality literature and young children together. After this happens, the attitudes start to change. Then I hear comments like "I was a big success with the 4-year-olds—they asked me to read it again!" or "Listen to this tape of my 3-year-old talking about his favorite book. It's exactly what we were discussing in class last week" or "My kindergartners really look forward to our story sessions. I'm convinced that picture books are a better way to develop reading abilities than workbooks and dittos."

You may not have had an opportunity to share picture books with children, or, conversely, you may have had extensive experience in bringing books and children together. Whatever your background, use *Young Children and Picture Books* to reflect upon your experience and to amass even richer experiences with children's literature. This book for teachers who are not already children's literature specialists is designed to enhance professional judgment about literature, to teach about children's literary responses, to explore the parent's role in children's literature, and to suggest ways of making literature an even more valuable resource in your classroom. Above all, it is my hope as an author that readers of *Young Children and Picture Books* will have a renewed appreciation for that category of literature uniquely well suited to the young child, the picture book.

Mary Renck Jalongo

Chapter 1
THE IMPORTANCE OF CHILDREN'S LITERATURE

*Only the rarest and best kind of
anything can be good enough for
the young.*

Walter de la Mare, Bells and Grass

In the fairy tale "Sleeping Beauty," the invited guests and god-
mothers bestow gifts upon the infant, bequests intended to ensure
the child's well-being. Early childhood educators also have a clear idea
of how to optimize the child's developmental journey from infancy
through maturity. Our ideas flesh out a prototype for the adult we
hope young children will become—someone who loves and is loved,
someone with insight and vision, someone who is confident and
competent. It would be difficult to challenge such worthy objectives,
but the best ways to achieve these goals remain controversial.

Children's literature can and should play an integral part in the
child's developmental journey (Bettelheim, 1976; Chukovsky, 1971;
Huck, 1979; Jacobs, 1965; Lamme, Cox, Matanzo, & Olson, 1980;
Mitchell, 1937, 1948, 1956; Oppenheim, Brenner & Boegehold,
1986). Through experiences with picture books, the young child can
develop socially, personally, intellectually, culturally, and aesthetically.
Books enable the newly socialized child to explore interpersonal
relationships and human motives. Picture books communicate self-ac-
ceptance and model coping strategies for children who are just learning to deal with powerful emotions. Literature also supplies information and raises questions, thus contributing to intellectual growth.
Through picture books, children meet families, settings, and cultures
that are in some ways similar and in some ways different from their
own. As a result, picture books contribute to the child's cultural
identity and multicultural awareness. Furthermore, because the picture
book is both illustrated and written, it simultaneously supports aesthetic development and growth in literacy.

Listen to Nikki, a 5-year-old, as she retells a fairy tale from the
Brothers Grimm. Notice how her aesthetic, cultural, social-emotional,

1

intellectual, and imaginative abilities all have been affected by her favorite book:

> Rumplestiltskin. One day there was a queen . . . that . . . and she was very pretty. One day, the miller's daughter came and they knew somebody, her daughter, that can do straw. So he took her to a room and she sat down and cried. And one time, the door sprang open and a little man walked in and he said, "Hi. What are you crying about?" "I have to spin all this into gold." And so, he said, "What will your give me if I do this into gold?" "My necklace." And he spun a-a-l-l-l the hay into gold. So one day she [was] put in a larger room. And so, the door sprang open *again* and the little man walked in. And he said, "What will your give me if you . . . if I spin it all *this* time?" "I'll give you the ring on my finger." So he took the ring on her finger and spinned all the hay into gold. That morning if she did another big larger room, they (the miller's daughter and the prince) would marry. So they took her to a larger room. So he sprang open *again* and if he . . . and he said, "What will your give me if I do it *now-ow?*" "I have nothing to give you." "Then you promise that I'll give you . . . that *you'll* give *me* the first baby that you have when you marry." So, one day they got married . . . and then she forgot about the little man. And he stepped in and he said, "All right. Give me your *chi-uld.*" And she was frightened 'cause she forgot about him. And so he said, "All right. I'll give you three days and if you remember my name, if you say my name, then you may keep your daughter . . . your son." So she's been thinkin' about all these names after day to day. And then one day she named *all* the names on the *list.* He said "no" to *all* of them that people gave her on her list. So one day she spied on him and he kept saying, "Rumplestiltskin is my name," riding on a spoon. So she went back and then she said, "Is your name Johnny? Jody? . . . In fact, your name is RUMPLESTILTSKIN!" And so *he* cri—he was *mad* on his *spoon*stick. So he flied away and she got to keep her baby. The end.

It was Paul O. Zelinsky's (1986) exquisite, jewel-toned oil paintings that first attracted Nikki's attention to this book. She likes the book because "it's pretty." Her favorite scene is the double-page painting of the wedding ceremony, a scene she also illustrated (page 3). Clearly, her aesthetic awareness has been affected by experiences with the book. The fact that the story takes place in a time and culture vastly different from her own enhances her cultural awareness. Consider, too, all the words she uses to describe emotions and motives. She has gained perspective on the possible consequences of a bargain struck in desperation and the universality of human emotions, something that contributes to her knowledge of self and others. She tells the story expressively, changing the tone of her voice to become different characters. Sometimes her voice sounds crafty, sometimes distressed, sometimes triumphant. Nikki's intellect is also enriched by this encounter with a picture book—she uses vocabulary and sentence structures that are far more complex than those required in routine conversations. Another intellectual achievement is her mastery of the

Nikki's depiction of the wedding scene from *Rumplestiltskin.*

basic story sequence. The book also stimulates Nikki's imagination. She can envision dynamic actions that cannot be fully represented in the freeze frame of a picture, such as the little man flying about, the straw being spun, or the door springing open. In this way, one book has been responsible for affecting imaginative, intellectual, cultural, social-emotional, and aesthetic development.

Author Jane Yolen (1977) is a particularly eloquent spokesperson for the contributions of literature to the child's development:

> Just as the child is born with a literal hole in its head, where the bones slowly close underneath the fragile shield of skin and hair, just so the child is born with a figurative hole in his heart. Slowly it too is filled up. . . . What slips in before it anneals creates the man or woman that child grows into. Literature, folklore, mythology — they surely must rank as one of the most important intrusions into the human heart. (p. 645)

Despite the importance of literature in children's lives, it can be ignored, neglected, or trivialized. In environments that do not support literature, teachers are unfamiliar with books published since their last children's literature course. Parents give up the struggle to find time to read to their children and soon even an occasional bedtime story is abandoned. Education majors feel foolish carrying copies of picture books around and defend their egos with complaints about "kiddie lit." College faculty sometimes equate quantity with appreciation. Then, instead of providing relevant experiences in sharing picture books with young children, they require students to write a hundred or more book reports. Each of these situations fails to explore the potential of the picture book.

How might these environments be changed in ways that support literature? The place to begin is with enjoyment:

> The proper satisfactions of reading, even in the newly literate child — even, indeed, in the non-literate story listening child — provide a robust affirmation of our common humanity, whether we are young or old, to understand and to be moved by and to gather ourselves the products of creative imagination. (Rosenheim, 1967, p. 13)

The satisfactions of literature should not be the province of a privileged few. Children are universally entitled to meaningful experiences with memorable books. As educators, we have an obligation to familiarize children with many different picture books *and* to convince adult skeptics about the benefits of children's experiences with literature. In order to meet this challenge successfully, early childhood professionals need to formulate clear, persuasive answers to these three questions:

What is literature?

What can children learn from literature?

How does literature meet the developmental needs of the young child?

A Definition for Literature

Observing young children and their books emphasizes the need for a broad definition of the picture book. Toddlers with a board book, preschoolers who sing along with a song picture book, and first graders who pore over a science book must all be accommodated by a definition for literature. In general, literature may be defined as "the imaginative shaping of life and thought into the forms and structures of language" (Huck, Hepler, & Hickman, 1987, p. 4).

Picture books, a special category of children's literature, are publications in which the pictures stand alone, the pictures dominate the text, or the words and illustrations are at least equally important (Sutherland & Hearne, 1977).

Usually the term *picture book* refers to picture *story* books, books that have simple plots and contain, on the average, about 200 words. These stories are written for children and (at least initially) shared with them by adults.

When Is a Book Literature?

The distinction between a picture book and other printed and illustrated material can best be made using a concrete example. Suppose there are several books in front of you. One is a routine coloring book on bicycle safety. The rest are children's books that have been well received by both adults and children. Contrasting the two types of publications makes the characteristics of literature apparent.

Attributes of Literature

Literature differs from other written and illustrated material in terms of its use of language; artistic quality; ways of depicting experience; and in content, form, and structure (Purves & Monson, 1984).

Use of language. In a typical coloring book, language is used in an obvious, literal way. It holds no surprises nor does it have a cadence or rhythm. The potential of language is not fully explored and the writing is not literary in any sense. Even literature in its simplest form does more with words than simply label the pictures. Consider, for example, *Chicken Soup With Rice,* Maurice Sendak's (1962) ode to a favorite food and delightful book of months. Here the language is lilting and captivating. It activates thought and creates images rather than simply labeling what is already apparent in the pictures. Few words are used and each word is chosen carefully.

Artistic quality. Quality picture books (with the exception of wordless books) include both art and language. In fact, it is the interplay of words and illustrations that makes a picture book a special category of literature. Children's book illustrators also use facing pages and the turning of pages to the best possible advantage (Bader, 1976) as the panoramic illustration from *Grandfather Twilight* (Berger, 1984) reveals. Picture book art does not simply depict a situation, it extends and complements the mood of language. *Grandfather Twilight* is a peaceful, magical bedtime story about a snowy-haired gentleman who is responsible for the gradual change from day to night. Nightfall, when explained in this way, somehow seems benevolent. The pictures do more than give a literal interpretation. They evoke an emotional response from readers or listeners and reward them with a reassuring myth. As Ciancolo (1984) observes, quality in picture book art requires illustrations

> . . . that are understandable, evoke emotional identification and intense emotional response, that allow room for the exercise of the reader's own imagination, that provide the reader with a new, wholesome (and vital) way of looking at the world and at life. (p. 847)

Contrast this with an illustration for a coloring book. It does just the opposite — it is a case of "what you see is what you get."

From *Grandfather Twilight* by Barbara Berger. Copyright © 1984 by Barbara Berger. Reprinted by permission of the publisher, Philomel/The Putnam Publishing Group.

Ways of depicting experience. All literature has a voice, a way of speaking to the reader, and a way of describing experience. Sometimes that voice speaks to the reader/listener through the dialogue of characters. At other times the voice is a sympathetic narrator who tells the story. In a coloring book, the reverse is true. The sparse text has no voice, no feeling that these words really are spoken by someone.

Contrast this with a book like *Bailey Goes Camping* (Henkes, 1985). When his older siblings, Bruce and Betty, get ready to go to camp, Bailey is told that he is "too little to go" and then reassured that "in a few years" he can. But that feeling of being excluded cannot be dismissed so lightly. Bruce and Betty have described a very inviting experience, one that involves swimming, sleeping in a tent, telling ghost stories, and roasting marshmallows. Young children share in Bailey's delight when, with the help of his parents, he manages to do all of these things right at home. This is another important attribute of literature. It is evocative. Literature pulls us in, involves us. Pre-schoolers who hear *Bailey Goes Camping* often respond with surprised laughter at a picture of Bailey wearing his sunglasses in the bathtub. When the story is finished, they often say "Read it again!" Responses like these are a testimonial to the book's evocativeness and ways of depicting experience.

The difference between literature and other printed material in book form is like the difference between singing a song and singing the alphabet. True, "The ABC Song" has some of the characteristics of music — a melody and a semblance of lyrics. But it really does not qualify as music in the fullest sense of the word. Similarly, if a picture book does not use language imaginatively, use art expressively, or depict experience authentically, it lacks some essential elements of literature.

Content, form, and structure. Picture books forge connections among the topics, the characters, the plot, the setting, the point of view, and the illustrations.

Quality children's books can have serious, as well as light-hearted, subjects. Consider, for example, a book like *The Patchwork Quilt* (Flournoy, 1985). The characters are family members, and the setting is their home. Realistic illustrations are well suited to the story's plot, which centers on the elderly grandmother's illness. She despairs of ever completing the quilt that she started, but her grand-daughter involves the entire family in completing the project and, in so doing, rekindles her grandmother's will to survive. In this story, content, form, and structure combine to convey a message of intergenerational understanding.

By the time most children are 5 years old, they already know key elements of story form (Applebee, 1978). They know that a story has a beginning, a middle, and an end; they use words like "Once there was . . ." or "The End" to reflect this knowledge. Young children also recognize structural elements of picture books such as repetition or rhyme. Thus, even those who are relatively new to literature perceive the literary attributes of content, form, and structure.

* * *

As we have seen, picture books differ from other types of written and illustrated material linguistically, artistically, experimentally, and structurally. How do these characteristics of literature make it a resource for children's learning?

From *Bailey Goes Camping* by Kevin Henkes. Copyright © 1985 by Kevin Henkes. Reprinted by permission of the publisher, Greenwillow Books (A division of William Morrow & Company, Inc.).

From *The Patchwork Quilt* by Valerie Flournoy. Illustration copyright © 1985 by Jerry Pinkey. Reprinted by permission of the publisher, Dial Books for Young Readers.

Learning Through Literature

Katz (1988) has identified four levels of learning fundamental to early childhood education: knowledge, skills, dispositions, and feelings. These categories of learning are directly applicable to experiences with literature. Even a single book can promote learning at all four levels. *Knowledge* is typically acquired through the senses, personal experience, or direct instruction. *Skills* are learned through practice. *Dispositions,* according to Katz, are "habits of mind." An example of a disposition would be curiosity, consulting a picture book to obtain information. Dispositions are acquired by observing models.

How do these three of Katz's categories relate to literacy? Learning to decipher words is the result of knowledge and skill. Wanting to read is a disposition. When young children realize that the text of a book they have heard so many times comes not from the person but from those black marks on the page, it is a revelation. Children want to be able to perform this magical feat. The child who has a disposition to read has observed others reading. One of the best ways for children to see literate adults in action is during picture book sharing sessions.

The fourth essential aspect of learning is *feelings,* the emotional tone of a learning experience: whether it is pressured or relaxed, competitive or cooperative, frustrating or enjoyable. The young child who associates warmth, closeness, and pleasure with picture books enters school with a tremendous advantage. Meek's (1982) studies of children who did not successfully learn to read led her to conclude that "if their earliest experience of learning at school imprints the idea that reading is hard work, they do not easily progress to the belief that it can be voluntarily engaged in for pleasure" (p. 290).

Thus, literacy seems to operate on the "iceberg principle" — knowledge and skills are only the tip of the iceberg. Dispositions and feelings are the substantial portion that lies beneath the surface. Emphasizing knowledge and skills to the virtual exclusion of dispositions and feelings results in an *aliterate* population. In other words, it produces learners who know how to read but refuse to read. Cullinan (1981) reports that although 94% of the nation is literate, only 55% of the literate population read *one* book within the previous year. This is yet another reason why an emphasis on the enjoyment of literature during the preschool years and primary grades is so important. "Literature, not reading lessons, teaches children to read in ways that no basal reader can, because literature is read, if at all, with passion, with desire" (Meek, 1982, p. 291).

This concept was pioneered at teacher education institutions such as the Bank Street College of Education and Columbia University Teachers College in the early years of the 20th Century. The belief that literature, not reading lessons, teaches children to read was at the core of nursery school, kindergarten, and primary grade literacy programs in Progressive schools across this country in the 1920s, 30s, 40s, and 50s. It has been the philosophy guiding the reading program in many excellent early childhood education classrooms and teacher preparation institutions ever since. Yet, in recent years, many schools have neglected literature in favor of lessons. They should remember that early familiarity with good books promotes literacy.

How are the feelings, dispositions, skills, and knowledge of literacy affected by early experiences with picture books? The following discussion between 5-year-old Leah and her librarian offers some insight. Leah has not merely learned *about* stories, she has made them her own, made them part of her daily life. She also has become quite a storyteller herself.

Leah: A 5-year-old learns through literature.

Leah (discussing *The Nutcracker,* Hoffmann, 1984): The little girl was named Clara . . . she, she was sick and she wore a blue party dress and her doctor gave her a nutcracker for Christmas. And her brother stamped on it. Well, her *godfather* gave her the nutcracker. And her brother stamped on it and kicked it and his godfather picked him up on the hair and pulled him out — *ordered* him out. Because he didn't like that. And she had a dream that it danced around and her nutcracker grew and grew and grew until it was a person. There was a beautiful ballet dancer named the Sugar Plum Fairy and she was all purple and there was a Castle of Sleeps and there was a jewelry box lady and the flowers were dancing and the bees and butterflies and see, the doctor had put some dolls out, some wind-up dolls and they *danced*. And you know what else? You know what I got for Christmas? . . . My Aunt June got me a ballet suit.

Librarian: A ballet suit?

Leah: Yeah! It came with a *tutu* and it came with the tights and the shirt and it came with ballet shoes.

Librarian: So, are you going to be a ballet dancer?

Leah: Well, yes, I *want* to . . . I got that book because Stacy gave it to me — our next door neighbor. And you know what? You haven't heard at all — I have a boyfriend . . . Derek. He was at school and he moved (lowers voice) to *Lima, Ohio.*

Librarian: Oh, no.

Leah: And you know what? Every ti — when he was at school, every time he saw I went, he always kissed my hand. And I WAS GETTING SICK OF IT! I *was.* And I thought . . . and one day when he was about to kiss my hand, I put my gloves on so he wouldn't. (laughs) He said, "How about kissing your cheek"? and I said, *"No way."* I thought: "Oh, no — I should have my scarf on!" (giggles) But I took my mittens off after that because he wanted to kiss my cheek. I don't like that at all, I really don't. He *always* did that. I keep *dreaming* of him every night. I miss him. And before he went — And you know what? I gave him a going-away present. I gave him a COMIC BOOK! . . . And I miss him now a lot, a whole lot. . . . Do you know the tape of Peter Wolf? I keep *dreaming* of that, and I kept *reading* about big bad wolfs. So every time when I dreamed of it, I snuggled up close because I was afraid that it would come and eat me so I snuggled up close to my Mama so it wouldn't. I thought that big bad wolf was *real* . . . sheesh!

Librarian: Do you think that now?

Leah: No, but one morning I dreamed about the story that you lent out one time about the little girl and the Gunniwolf.

Librarian: Oh, the puppet show that we did here. Did that scare you?

Leah: Oh, not that much. Know what? Now they're showing it on television . . . but the Gunniwolf, it looked real funny—it looked like a *spider!* (laughs) The little girl was a Black little girl and she got some yellowish and white flowers and yellow flowers and she dropped all of them and she got some orange flowers and she dropped all of them and she got home and her mother told her stay out of the woods and she got home and she *cried.* And her mother went away at the end of the book. She went in there because she saw some flowers. She thought they were nice for her Mama and she just *almost* got eaten. But she didn't. (laughs) Yeah, that's the whole story!

Where knowledge and skills are concerned, Leah clearly has been influenced by literature. She has acquired new vocabulary (for example, "stamped" and "ordered") and is good at telling a story. Her favorite stories have had an effect on her dispositions as well. She has borrowed books from the library, listened to tapes, attended a puppet performance, and even critiqued a film version of *The Gunniwolf* (Harper, 1967), which is an earlier version of *Red Riding Hood* (Marshall, 1987). Additionally, Leah has used literature as a safe way of confronting one of the most prevalent fears of preschoolers, a fear of animals. So her experiences with literature have deeply affected all aspects of her life. Children need literature, as Robert Lawson (quoted in Allen, 1967) has said, "for the chuckles . . . the gooseflesh . . the glimpses of glory."

What Can Children Learn From Literature?

Children benefit from experience with literature in many ways. Through meaningful experiences with picture books, children learn (Hennings, 1986):

- to appreciate excellence in the writing and illustrations represented in books (Kiefer, 1985)
- to interpret and evaluate literature in its many different forms (Roser & Martinez, 1985)
- to communicate more effectively by incorporating the content, vocabulary, and linguistic complexity found in literature (Solsken, 1985)
- to broaden their perspective to view the different cultures and individuals in less stereotypic ways (Sims, 1982)
- to select books that suit their interests (Hepler & Hickman, 1982)

Literature and the Young Child's Developmental Needs

Literature does more than teach the child, as important as that goal may be. It also contributes to the young child's development in a variety of ways (Glazer, 1986; Hepler & Hickman, 1982; Schlager, 1978). Figure 1.1 summarizes children's language development and literary needs and the ways picture books can satisfy those needs.

A wonderful resource for matching children's developmental stages with appropriate picture books is *Choosing Books for Kids* (Oppenheim, Brenner, & Boegehold, 1986). This book discusses each stage of development from infancy through adolescence and gives annotated book suggestions for each stage. It also lists for each age 10 books that should not be missed!

What is the best where literature is concerned? Choices in picture books have long-term significance in children's lives. Ideally,

> Books do for children the same things they do for adults: they inform, they stimulate, delight, amuse, and transport us all into other worlds of thought and experience. Most importantly, they make us think and feel and respond, and they put us in intimate touch with the best that has been known and thought. ("A Note to Grownups," 1985)

Choosing the best literature and sharing it effectively with children: That is what the remainder of this book is about.

References

A note to grownups. (1985). *Picture Book Studio Journal I*. Natick, MA: Picture Book Studio.

Allen, A. T. (1967, December). Literature for children: An engagement with life. *The Horn Book Magazine, 43*, pp. 732–737.

Applebee, A. N. (1978). *A child's concept of story: Ages two to five*. Chicago: University of Chicago Press.

Bader, B. (1976). *American picture books from* Noah's Ark *to* The Beast Within. New York: Macmillan.

Bettelheim, B. (1976). *The uses of enchantment: The meaning and importance of fairy tales*. New York: Knopf.

Chukovsky, K. (1971). *From two to five* (M. Morton, Trans.). Berkeley, CA: University of California. (Original work published 1963)

Ciancolo, P. (1984). Illustrations in children's books. In Z. Sutherland & M. C. Livingston (Eds.), *The Scott, Foresman anthology of children's literature* (pp. 846–878) Glenview, IL: Scott, Foresman.

Cullinan, B. (1981). *Literature and the child*. New York: Harcourt Brace Jovanovich.

Glazer, J. (1986). *Literature for young children*. Columbus, OH: Merrill.

Hennings, D. G. (1986). *Communication in action*. Boston: Houghton Mifflin.

Hepler, S. J., & Hickman, J. (1982). "The book was okay. I love you." Social aspects of responses to literature. *Theory Into Practice, 21*, 278–283.

Huck, C. S. (1979). *Children's literature in the elementary school*. New York: Holt, Rinehart & Winston.

Huck, C. S., Hepler, S. J., & Hickman, J. (1987). *Children's literature in the elementary school*. New York: Holt, Rinehart & Winston.

Figure **1.1**
Chronology of Language Development and Literary Needs in Early Childhood

Approximate age	Language development	Literary needs
birth – 6 mos.	comforted by soft sounds; cries, gurgles, and coos	to hear rhythmic language, rhymes, chants, songs
6 – 9 mos.	produces one-syllable sounds; sounds develop intonation patterns; may attempt to imitate "Ma" and "Da"	All of the above plus: to participate in using repetitious books, point-and-say books, books that pose simple questions, books that have clear pictures of familiar objects, simple stories with predictable plots
9 mos. – 1 yr. 6 mos.	responds to some words; begins using holophrases (one-word utterances) like "doggie," "juice," "ball"; unusual pronunciation may make the child's words difficult to understand	
1 yr. 6 mos. – 2 yrs.	points to objects, vocabulary of 20 to 200 words; understands simple questions; uses telegraphic speech like "Daddy bye-bye"	
2 yrs. – 2 yrs. 6 mos.	50 – 400 word vocabulary; continuance of two- and three-word phrases; begins using pronouns and prepositions but may get them confused (saying "inside" when meaning "outside," for example)	All of the above plus: to respond to simple stories that can be dramatized, stories that include families, important changes, interesting characters, predictable outcomes
2 yrs. 6 mos. – 3 yrs.	three- and four-word utterances; uses correct word order more often; applies some grammatical rules; comprehends better; is more intelligible to others; asks questions like "What's that?"	All of the above plus: to enjoy simple counting rhymes and songs, answering questions, repetition of captivating phrases
3 – 4 yrs.	1,000 word vocabulary; better articulation of certain sounds (s, th, z, r, l); more complex sentences and questions, beginning conversation	All of the above plus: to retell or memorize stories, to use characters and situations from literature in sociodramatic play
4 – 5 yrs.	1,500 – 1,800 words; correctly names many objects, actions, colors, etc.; may be able to identify some letters or read simple words; can converse with other children and adults	All of the above plus: to memorize favorite stories and "read" them; to sustain interest in stories with more plot and character development; to enjoy stories that explore basic concepts, human emotions, and relationships; and to distinguish between real/make-believe or good/bad behavior

Note: Based on Lamme, Cox, Matanzo, & Oslon (1980) and Papalia & Olds (1986).

Jacobs, L.B. (1965). *Using literature with young children*. New York: Teachers College Press, Columbia University.

Katz, L. (1988). What should young children be doing? *American Educator, 12,* 28–33, 44.

Kiefer, B. (1985, November/December). Looking beyond picture book preferences. *The Horn Book Magazine,* pp. 705–713.

Lamme, L.L., Cox, V., Matanzo, J., & Olson, M. (1980). *Raising readers: A guide to sharing literature with young children.* New York: Walker.

Meek, M. (1982). *Learning to read.* London: Bodley Head.

Mitchell, L.S. (Ed.). (1937). *Another here and now story book.* New York: Dutton.

Mitchell, L.S. (Ed.). (1948). *Here and now story book, two- through seven-year-olds.* New York: Dutton.

Mitchell, L.S. (1956). *Believe and make believe.* New York: Dutton.

Oppenheim, J., Brenner, B., & Boegehold, B.O. (1986). *Choosing books for kids.* New York: Ballantine.

Papalia, D., & Olds, S.W. (1986). *A child's world: Infancy through adolescence.* New York: McGraw-Hill.

Purves, A.C., & Monson, D.L. (1984). *Experiencing children's literature.* Glenview, IL: Scott, Foresman.

Rosenheim, E. (1967). Children's reading and adult's values. In S. Fenwick (Ed.), *A critical approach to children's literature* (pp. 3–14). Chicago: University of Chicago Press.

Roser, N., & Martinez, M. (1985). Roles adults play in preschoolers' response to literature. *Language Arts, 62,* 485–490.

Schlager, N. (1978). Predicting children's choices in literature: A developmental approach. *Children's Literature in Education, 9,* 136–142.

Sims, R. (1982). *Shadow and substance: Afro-American experience in contemporary children's fiction.* Urbana, IL: National Council of Teachers of English.

Solsken, J.W. (1985). Authors of their own learning. *Language Arts, 62,* 491–499.

Sutherland, Z., & Hearne, B. (1977, October). In search of the perfect picture book definition. *Wilson Library Bulletin,* pp. 158–160.

Yolen, J. (1977). How basic is shazam? *Language Arts, 54,* 645–651.

Children's Books

Berger, B. (1984). *Grandfather twilight.* New York: Philomel.

Flournoy, V. (1985). *The patchwork quilt.* New York: Dial.

Harper, W. (1967). *The gunniwolf.* New York: Dutton.

Henkes, K. (1985). *Bailey goes camping.* New York: Greenwillow.

Hoffmann, E.T.A. (1984). *The nutcracker.* New York: Crown. (Originally published in 1820)

Marshall, J. (1987). *Red riding hood.* New York: Dial.

Sendak, M. (1962). *Chicken soup with rice.* New York: Harper & Row.

Zelinsky, P.O. (1986). *Rumplestiltskin.* New York: Dutton.

For Further Reading

Burke, E. (1990). *Literature for the young child.* Boston, MA: Allyn & Bacon.

Cambourne, B. (1988). *The whole story.* Sydney, Australia: Ashton/Scholastic.

Ciancolo, P.J. (1990). *Picture books for children.* Chicago, IL: American Library Association.

Jalongo, M.R. (1992). *Early childhood language arts.* Boston, MA: Allyn & Bacon.

Kulleseid, E.R., & Strickland, D.S. (1990). *Literature, literacy, and learning: Classroom teachers, library media specialists, and the literature-based curriculum.* Chicago, IL: American Library Association.

Norton, D.E. (1991). *Through the eyes of a child: Introduction to children's literature.* Columbus, OH: Merrill.

Raines, S.C., & Canady, R. (1989). *Story s-t-r-e-t-c-h-e-r-s.* Mt. Rainier, MD: Gryphon House.

Raines, S.C., & Canady, R. (1990). *More story s-t-r-e-t-c-h-e-r-s.* Mt. Rainier, MD: Gryphon House.

Shulevitz, U. (1989). What is a picture book? *The Five Owls, 2*(4), 49–53.

Chapter 2
WHAT IS QUALITY LITERATURE?

While good literature often teaches, it goes beyond the functions of informing, entertaining, and providing emotional release; it exists in its own right as an art.

Eileen Tway, Reading Ladders for Human Relations

Arriving at a definition for quality is exceedingly difficult. Why is anything more valued or worthwhile than something else? The picture book is an artistic form, so the same basic criteria that are used to evaluate sculpture or music apply to picture books. Art is valuable when it is judged to be exceptional in some way, when it retains its value over time, when it is recognized as art by the culture, and/or when it is produced by someone who is considered to be an artist.

Where children's books are concerned, this means that the book is reviewed favorably or perhaps wins awards. Ideally, the book endures as a favorite and satisfies critics, adults, and children. As is the case with other classics, certain authors and illustrators consistently emerge as better than others (see Appendix A).

Despite these general guidelines, the task of defining quality in picture books remains a challenge:

> The question of what is good is a dangerous one. The appellation of
> "good" is a fragile raft of opinion resting precariously on the
> shifting quicksand of taste. What is acclaimed today may be ignored
> or criticized only a few years hence. Obviously one answer to the
> problem is to wait until a book has stood the test of time before
> declaring it good. (Stewig, 1980, p. 10)

As our sensibilities change, our concepts of what is suitable for children and what represents quality are altered. It is only recently, for example, that picture book characters with disabilities like *My Friend Leslie* (Rosenberg, 1983) have been widely accepted. Some books that were once very popular, like *Little Black Sambo* (Bannerman, 1923), have virtually disappeared because by today's standards or political climate they seem to some to perpetuate offensive stereotypes. So the passage of time, cultural and political influences, and individual preferences affect prevailing concepts of quality in children's literature.

According to Bank Street College of Education's children's literature experts William H. Hooks and Claudia Lewis:

> There is a powerful body of writing loosely known as "classics of children's literature." As a rule these writings cut across several stages of childhood, and many would be considered to be for all ages, defying any attempt to age relate them. They are pieces of writing characterized by fine style, originality of concept, and universal appeal. They have withstood the test of time and remain fresh and vigorous as each new generation meets and is refreshed by them. (Oppenheim, Brenner, & Boegehold, 1986, p. 301)

Formulating Professional Judgments About Picture Books

Even though selecting a quality picture book may be difficult, it needs to be done, and done frequently. Parents and teachers must decide which of the many books on library or bookstore shelves is written and illustrated better than others. According to children's book sales figures, more adults are making these decisions all of the time. Sales of children's hardbound books went from 298.1 million in 1981 to 663 million in 1986. Defining quality in picture books poses some of the same challenges as describing masterful teaching. It is almost easier to say what it is not than to define what it is. In *The Way To Write for Children,* Aiken (1982) says that a good children's book

> . . . is not something that can be dashed off to schedule, turned off a production belt like a piece of factory goods. It should not be anything with an axe to grind, propaganda for something, a hidden sales message. It should not be perfunctory, meaningless, flat, coy or second rate. (p. 15)

If a good picture book is none of the above, then what is it? The first step in understanding decisions about quality is to recognize that many different people exert an influence on the process: children, parents, teachers, and professionals in the field of children's literature. Each of these groups has an important influence on the picture book.

Professionals in the field of children's literature — picture book authors, illustrators, children's book editors, and reviewers — affect what is published. Authors determine which manuscripts will be submitted, editors decide which ones will be published, and those who review children's literature can choose to praise, overlook, or criticize a book.

Parents influence children's literature by deciding which books to share with their child—which books to borrow from the library, and which books to buy.

The *child* affects adults' ideas about good books through his or her individual response to literature. If a child does not appear interested in a particular book, the adult will try another book that is more appealing or perhaps try the same book at another time. In this way, the child's response affects both current and future book selections by adults.

Professionals who share literature with children include teachers, librarians, and teacher educators. Their uses, endorsements, and purchases of picture books help to determine whether the book will emerge as a classic.

The enduring success of a particular picture book is a complex interaction of these people and variables.

From Hans Christian Andersen, *The Ugly Duckling*, retold by Marianna Mayer, illustrated by Thomas Locker. Illustration copyright © 1987 by Thomas Locker. Reproduced with permission of Macmillan Publishing Company.

How Difficult Is It To Write a Children's Book?

Talk to aspiring writers and they will often say that they want to begin by writing a children's book. Why? Because it is presumed to be much easier than writing for adults. Before agreeing with this idea, consider the following information:

- A good picture book must appeal not only to the child but also to adults who purchase and read stories to children. Publishers, parents, librarians, teachers, and critics are often the book's first audience, children the second.

- The book must grab the young child's interest initially and maintain interest through repeated readings; it can be simple but not trivial or condescending.

- Although the number of words will probably range from none to 1,000, any words used must be selected carefully because the book will be read aloud like poetry.

- Many children's book authors are also artists. If an author writes the text for a picture book and a publisher accepts it, the publisher will assign an artist to the project. Even though picture book authors are not required to be illustrators as well, they often are. It is one way of ensuring that the text and the illustrations that the author imagined are perfectly matched.

- The typical picture book is 25 pages of actual text on a 6″ × 9″ paper size. It will contain an average of 100 to 400 words. Within these constraints, a picture book author needs to accomplish such worthy goals as informing, enlightening, entertaining, and stimulating the imagination of the young child (Roberts, 1984).

- Of all the children's books ever published, there are only about 40,000 children's books currently in print (Huck, Hepler & Hickman, 1987). The chances that your book will remain in print and be selected year after year by large numbers of children are very small.

- Year after year, the list of the great books for children remains relatively unchanged (Aiken, 1982). With more than 2,500 new picture books published each year (Lukens, 1984), an author's chance of creating the Great American Picture Book is about .0004 percent.

- The typical child reads only about 600 books during an entire childhood. Ideally, each book should enrich children's lives "with new ideas, insight, humor or vocabulary" (Aiken, 1982, p. 10). This requirement is perhaps the most intimidating of all. How many authors and illustrators can hope to contribute to children's lives in a significant way?

Talk to the more than 10,000 aspiring writers who have attended the Bank Street Writer's Lab begun over 50 years ago (1936) by Lucy Sprague Mitchell and still offering children's book writing labs and workshops year round, and you will hear how much more is involved in writing a high-quality picture book than you ever imagined! The book *Writing for Young Children* (Lewis, 1981) will help you understand how it is done.

Deciding Which Books Are Good

Eventually, those who choose literature for children must rely upon good instincts, which result from thorough and frequent examination of the best that literature has to offer (Hearne, 1981). As early as 1882, when the first guide to children's books was published (M. J. Roggenbuck, personal communication with Polly Greenberg, 1988), people knowledgeable about children's literature have been trying to choose the best. Evaluating children's literature is like appraising the worth of anything from breakfast cereal to the family car — we study the features, do some comparison shopping, and establish evaluation criteria prior to reaching a decision (see Figures 2.1 and 2.2). We also consider the needs and personality of the individual and try to match the child with the best possible books.

Figure 2.1
How To Select a Picture Book

Elleman (1986) has devised a four-step system to select a picture book:

Step 1 — Quickly look over the book to get a feel for the tone and approach.

Step 2 — Read just the text, mentally blocking out the art.

Step 3 — Read the story carefully while focusing on the harmony of words and pictures, backtracking and pausing whenever you feel like it.

Step 4 — Carefully look at other details such as book design, paper, type, endpapers, dedications, etc.

Some questions to consider include:

What is the illustrator attempting to do?

Why is a certain effect used? Is it successful?

Are the illustrations or photographs aesthetically pleasing and of good quality?

Are story and picture well integrated?

Is there flow from page to page?

Has the artist considered the constraints of format?

Has the child been kept in mind? What age child?

Could a young child get a sense of the basic concepts of story sequence by looking at the pictures?

What about balance, harmony, mood, composition, line, and color?

Note: Based on Elleman (1986).

Educators can select a good picture book by reading the reviews, discussing it with others, and reading it themselves. With approximately 2,500 new picture books published each year, it is unrealistic to assume that every early childhood educator can obtain, much less read and evaluate, them all. One way of knowing which books children like is by asking a children's librarian (see Appendix B for some recommendations from the American Library Association). Another way is to consult published reviews of picture books (Figure 2.3). The next step is to borrow picture books every week, share them with children, and give children the opportunity to find their favorites. A sense of quality in literature, then, is acquired by surrounding children and adults with the best until mediocre and poor picture books are no longer appealing.

Figure 2.2
Evaluation Questions for Picture Books in Early Childhood Education

General evaluation questions

1. Does the book compare favorably with other picture books of its type?
2. Has the picture book received the endorsements of professionals?
3. Are the literary elements of plot, theme, character, style, and setting used effectively?
4. Do the pictures complement the story?
5. Is the story free from ethnic, racial, or sex-role stereotypes?
6. Is the picture book developmentally appropriate for the child?
7. Do preschoolers respond enthusiastically to the book?
8. Is the topic (and the book's treatment of it) suitable for the young child?
9. Does the picture book appeal to the parent or teacher?

Additional evaluation questions for illustrations

1. Are the illustrations and text synchronized?
2. Does the mood conveyed by the artwork (humorous/serious, rollicking/quiet) complement that of the story?
3. Are the illustrative details consistent with the text?
4. Could a child get a sense of the basic concepts or story sequence by looking at the pictures?
5. Are the illustrations or photographs aesthetically pleasing?
6. Is the printing (clarity, form, line, color) of good quality?
7. Can children view and re-view the illustrations, each time getting more from them?
8. Are the illustrative style and complexity suited to the age level of the intended audience?

Note: Based on Huck (1979).

Figure **2.3**
Selected Sources for Reviews of Picture Books

Journals and magazines		
American Library Association	*School Library Journal* and *Booklist*	
Association for Childhood Education International	*Childhood Education*	
Council on Interracial Books for Children	*Interracial Books for Children Bulletin*	
Horn Book, Incorporated	*The Horn Book Magazine*	regularly reviews picture books in a section of the journal or magazine, publishes articles about children's literature, and/or publishes books about children's literature for teachers and parents
Human Sciences Press	*Day Care and Early Education*	
International Reading Association	*The Reading Teacher*	
National Association for the Education of Young Children	*Young Children*	
National Council of Teachers of English	*Language Arts* and *Bulletin of the Children's Literature Assembly*	
Allen Raymond, Incorporated	*Early Years*	
University of Chicago	*Bulletin of the Center for Children's Books*	
Newspapers		
New York Times	*New York Times Literary Supplement*	children's book reviews supplement published annually
Annotated bibliographies		
R. R. Bowker Company	*Best Books for Children* and other annotated bibliographies	
National Council of Teachers of English	*Adventuring With Books* and *Reading Ladders for Human Relations*	
Indexes of reviews		
Gale Research Publishing	*Book Review Index* and *Children's Literature Reviews*	synthesizes major children's book reviews published in a variety of sources
Publishing companies		
various publishing companies such as Dial, Harper & Row, and Putnam	*Trade Publishers Annual*	publishers' catalogues bound into large volumes; each catalogue advertises that company's award-winning books

Selecting Books Without Racial, Ethnic, or Gender Stereotypes

Literature has the power to influence ideas and expectations. This can be illustrated by the fact that when any group wants to control others completely, they burn or ban books that challenge their views. Because literature exerts such influence on children's perceptions, it is important to choose books that treat women, minorities, and other cultures fairly: "Young children are the most vulnerable to stereotypes and bias in books because books play a major role in shaping children's first images of the larger society" (Chambers, 1983, pp. 91–92).

What is a stereotype? A filmstrip from the Council on Interracial Books for Children (1978) defines a stereotype as follows:

> A stereotype is an oversimplified, generalized image describing all individuals in a group as having the same characteristics, that is to say, in appearance, in behavior, in beliefs. While there may be a germ of truth in a stereotype, the image usually represents a gross distortion, or an exaggeration of that truth, and has offensive, dehumanizing implications.

Campbell and Wirtenberg (1980) offer the following questions for assessing stereotypes in children's books:

- *Are people of different cultures and ethnic groups accurately portrayed?*

The illustrations in some books include offensive stereotypes such as Mexicans asleep under their sombreros. In other, less blatant examples of unsuitable portrayals, publishers will conform to the demand for multicultural materials by simply including one token character of a different race or different ethnic background. In the 1960s, some publishers simply shaded the faces of one character with obviously Caucasian features a different color! All of these practices subvert the goal of expanding children's cultural and ethnic awareness (Kendall, 1983).

- *Are girls and women portrayed as active and successful?*

Children's books sometimes suggest that females are intellectually inferior and basically subservient to males. Studies of children's books suggest that boy characters in active roles far outnumber girls (Yawkey & Yawkey, 1976). Beware of books that portray women as helpless, needing male protection or intervention in order to succeed. These books encourage dependency in girls and dominance in boys.

- *In stories with adult characters, do the authority figures include women and minorities?*

Typically, books about hospitals contain female nurses and White male doctors; books about schools usually portray female teachers and male administrators. Children need to see many different role models in order to get a sense of the wide range of possibilities for

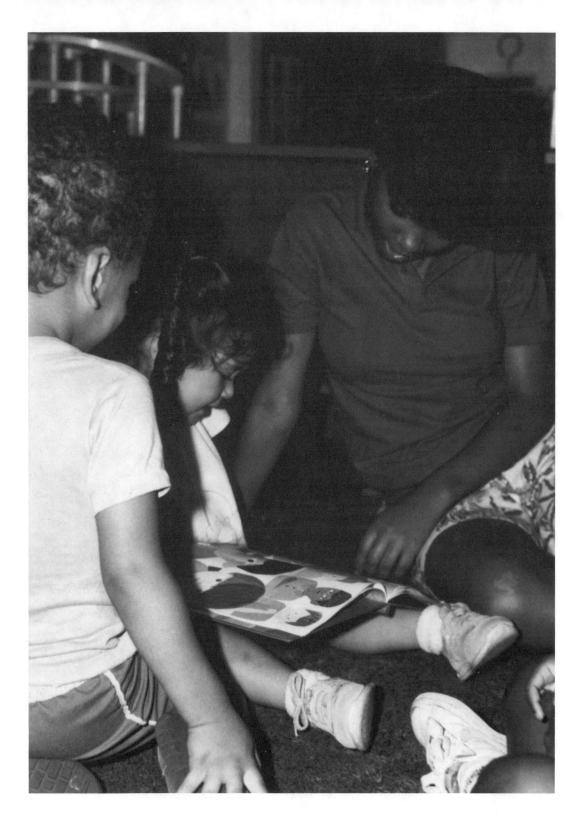

themselves. In the 1960s, concerned Black, Mexican-American, Asian, Native American, and other minority groups pointed out that children's concepts of various occupations and their personal aspirations are greatly influenced by the models they see in person, in books, and in films. In the 1970s, women's groups did the same thing. Recent research suggests that this is true (Hageman & Gladding, 1983).

- *Are families portrayed in all their diversity?*

Too many books for children convey the message that a family is defined as a mother, a father, and children. Presenting this family configuration suggests to the child that a single-parent family, an extended family, a stepfamily, a two-mother or two-father family, or another family grouping is inferior.

- *Do picture books depicting other cultures show only strange and exotic settings and people?*

Children need to identify with people who are different from themselves to become aware of their common humanity (Ravitch & Finn, 1987). When groups of people are depicted stereotypically, children acquire inaccurate impressions. Portrayals of Native Americans are a good example. Because the American Indian is usually shown in a headdress of feathers and living in a tipi during the 1800s, children often believe that there are no Native Americans among their contemporaries.

A book that allows children to glimpse another culture should highlight the universality of human emotions, motives, and experience. When differences are emphasized and these common bonds are ignored, children tend to see other cultures as quaint or bizarre. Ask an elementary school child to draw or describe a peer from Holland and the probable result is a person in wooden clogs surrounded by tulips and windmills. When books perpetuate stereotypes, they hinder the child's ability to identify with other people. Appendix C contains a bibliography of books that celebrate diversity and the universality of human experience.

The Child's Perspective on Quality

Every educator has at one time or another presented an award-winning picture book to children only to discover that this object of rave reviews from literary critics was panned by its primary audience. With all the frustration of parents at Christmas time who purchase an expensive toy and watch their child play delightedly with the wrappings, professionals who evaluate, purchase, and share children's literature are occasionally disappointed by children's responses to a book. It is sometimes true that those books selected by adult critics as outstanding are not the most popular with children (Nilsen, Peterson, and Searfoss, 1980). One college student enrolled in an undergraduate children's literature course encountered this situation firsthand. She had enlisted the help of her 4-year-old daughter to locate the gold and silver embossed seals of Caldecott and Newbery award-winning picture books at the local library. After several such library visits the preschooler remarked: "You find the ones with the stickers on them, Mommy. I want to get some *good* books."

How does this happen? Why might adults' and young children's preferences differ? Actually, there are several logical explanations for discrepancies in children's and adult's choices.

Availability/familiarity. Young children may not have access to quality literature. They may learn to prefer what is advertised just as they might learn to prefer junk food they see on commercials over a well-balanced meal. As a result, children might select books that are actually commercials for popular toys or syndicated cartoon characters because those characters are familiar. Children see them on television, on clothing, on food items, and on every imaginable store purchase from a school lunch box to vitamins.

Inexperience. Appearances can be deceiving, and young children must truly judge a book by its cover until an adult reads the book to them. Picture books require interaction between an adult and a child. Surrounding children with books is not enough. They need caring adults to invite them into the world of literature; they need someone to show them the way (Prescott, 1965).

The Story of Jumping Mouse by John Steptoe (1984) is a good example. It is a rich and complex Native American legend, one that a child would need to hear and discuss many times before mastering it. On page 29 is an excerpt from 5-year-old Anna's retelling of the story. Note that Anna has internalized the story structure even though this is a very challenging book.

Anna became intrigued by this challenging story because adults took the time to read it to her and to answer her questions. The mythical aspects of the story captured her imagination and, with repeated readings, it became her favorite book. A child without such opportunities could not unlock the potential of this book.

The Story of Jumping Mouse*
(Steptoe, 1984)

Text of the book	Anna, 5 years old
Once there was a young mouse who lived in the brush near a great river. During the day he and the other mice hunted for food. At night they gathered to hear the old ones tell stories. The young mouse like to hear about the desert beyond the river, and he got shivers from the stories about the dangerous shadows that lived in the sky. But his favorite was the tale of the far-off land.	(Anna reads title) The Mice by John Step. I'm holding it here. Sit where you guys can see. (Anna points to the page and says) Right here. (Pointing to the mouse) The little mice — that's a picture of the little mice.
The far-off land sounded so wonderful that young mouse began to dream about it. He knew he would never be content until he had been there. The old ones warned that the journey would be long and perilous, but the young mouse would not be swayed. He set off one morning before the sun risen.	One morning the little mouse went out to see the leaves, but it was raining, not raining hard. One morning he went out running in the forest 'cause he wanted to see what he could see.
It was evening before he reached the edge of the brush. Before him was the river; on the other side was the desert. The young mouse peered into the deep water: "How will I ever get across?" he said in dismay.	He was tired of his city. He saw a pond. (Anna raises the pitch of her voice to sound like the mouse) How will I ever get across the pond?
"Don't you know how to swim?" called a gravelly voice. The young mouse looked around and saw a small green frog. "Hello," he said. "What is swim?" "This is swimming," said the frog, and she jumped into the river.	A frog speaked to him.
"Oh," said the young mouse. "I don't think I can do that." "Why do you need to cross the river?" asked the frog, hopping back up the bank. "I want to go to the far-off land," said the young mouse. "It sounds too beautiful to live a lifetime and not see it.". . .	(Again, in her high-pitched tone of voice) Hello, Mrs. Frog. I would like to get across to see the rest of the city. . . .

Later, the rabbits will patter into your yard and eat pieces of your fallen apples. But only when they think you are asleep.

Poor selections by adults. Of course, adults can be misguided in *their* book choices and inflict those preferences on children. Sometimes adults approach picture books with a "Take this, it's good for you" mentality. Usually these "good for you" books are one of three types: (1) sermons disguised as picture books, which extoll the virtues of blind obedience to authority, (2) workbooks disguised as picture books, which emphasize drill and memorization of academic skills, or (3) syrupy children's books that reflect an adult's highly sentimentalized view of childhood. Furthermore, adults (like children) may seek familiar, widely advertised cartoon characters. The main difference is that adults will tend to prefer the characters reminiscent of their own childhoods — Mickey Mouse rather than the Transformers, for instance.

Developmental differences. It is sometimes difficult for an audience at one stage of development (adulthood) to respond as an audience at other stages of development (childhood). In Greenlaw's (1983) study of nearly 10,000 children, humorous books were the first choice of children in the primary grades, yet few humorous books ever earn adult acclaim. Even when we know that young children generally appreciate slapstick, role reversals, and incongruities, it is the rare adult who appreciates the child's sense of humor and can predict what children will consider funny (Jalongo, 1985). This difference in adult's and children's perspectives can account for some discrepancies in book preferences.

Social and temporal influences. Adult critics may identify a book as a landmark in children's literature because it is timely or remarkably different. The 1976 Caldecott winner *Why Mosquitoes Buzz in People's Ears,* written by Verna Aardema and illustrated by Leo and Diane Dillon, is a good example. The African influence on the story and art of the book filled a gap in existing children's literature and moved it forward. Considerations such as these often influence adults' choices. They may base decisions upon comparisons with other publications or intuition about the long-term significance of a book. Children, on the other hand, are new to the world of books. They will respond in a much more direct and immediate way.

Kiefer (1985) suggests the best resolution to this issue: "Rather than argue about whether to give children books which are good for them or books which we think they will like, perhaps we ought to ask how it is that children come to love the books which are good for them" (p. 706). How does this occur?

Books That Children Love

The Comic Adventures of Old Mother Hubbard and Her Dog (de Paola, 1981) is 4-year-old Leon's favorite book because "it has funny pictures."

A House Is a House for Me (Hoberman, 1979) is 5-year-old Suzanna's current choice "because it has words in, that when you say one word, the other one rhymes with it."

Teresa, a kindergartner, read *Happy Birthday, Moon* (Asch, 1981) "because my birthday's coming up. That's the reason I picked it out!"

When children "connect" with a picture book, it attracts them with the same magnetism as a song that causes a busy toddler to stop and listen with complete concentration. What do adults say when a novel is too good to miss? "I couldn't put it down!" The same holds true for a young child's favorite book, only in a much more literal sense. An adult puts a treasured book in a briefcase or on a bedside table, a child carries or drags it around everywhere; an adult rereads and underlines the not-to-be-forgotten passages, the young child scrutinizes and touches pictured objects. Literature is a paradox in that it seems to rivet us to each page yet moves us forward with the lure of what happens next. In ways that are sometimes grand and in ways that are sometimes small, the reader is better for having experienced a good book. Quality picture books have enough substance to fascinate a child even after repeated encounters with the same story.

A preschooler hears *Morris's Disappearing Bag* (Wells, 1975) for the first time and derives the meaning of words like "invisible" and "disappear." She hears it a second time and examines the pictures closely to find out more about the Christmas presents each of the three siblings receives. She hears it a third time and takes delight in the youngest child's triumph over an older brother and sister who try to exclude the baby of the family with those hurtful words "You're too little to play." And after the fourth reading, she imagines what it would be like to own a disappearing bag by announcing to the family, "I'm pretending to be invisible, so don't see me, okay?" In this way, a single story has been responsible for grabbing the attention, educating the mind, affecting the emotions, and stimulating the imagination. This is a quality book. It delights children and adults. It deserves to be called literature.

References

Aiken, J. (1982). *The way to write for children.* New York: St. Martin's.

Campbell, P. B., & Wirtenberg, J. (1980). How books influence children: What the research shows. *Interracial Books for Children Bulletin, 11*(6), 3.

Chambers, B. (1983). Counteracting racism and sexism in children's books. In O. Saracho & B. Spodek (Eds.), *Understanding the multicultural experience in early childhood education* (pp. 91–105). Washington, DC: NAEYC.

Council on Interracial Books for Children. (1978). *Identifying racism and sexism in children's books* [Filmstrip]. New York: Racism and Sexism Resource Center for Educators (distributor).

Elleman, B. (1986). Picture book art: Evaluation. *Booklist, 82,* 1548.

Greenlaw, M. J. (1983). Reading interest research and children's choices. In N. Reser & M. Frith (Eds.), *Children's choices: Teaching with books children like* (pp. 90–119). Newark, DE: International Reading Association.

Hageman, M., & Gladding, S. (1983). The art of career exploration: Occupational and sex-role stereotyping among elementary school children. *Elementary School Guidance and Counseling, 18,* 280–287.

Hearne, B. (1981). *Choosing books for children: A common sense guide.* New York: Delacorte.

Huck, C. (1979). *Children's literature in the elementary school.* New York: Holt, Rinehart & Winston.

Huck, C., Hepler, S., & Hickman, J. (1987). *Children's literature in the elementary school.* New York: Holt, Rinehart & Winston.

Jalongo, M. R. (1985). Children's literature: There's some sense to its humor. *Childhood Education, 62,* 109–114.

Kendall, F. (1983). *Diversity in the classroom: A multicultural approach to the education of young children.* New York: Teachers College Press, Columbia University.

Kiefer, B. (1985, November/December). Looking beyond picture book preferences. *The Horn Book Magazine,* pp. 705–713.

Lewis, C. (1981). *Writing for young children.* Garden City, NY: Anchor Press/Doubleday.

Lukens, R. (1984). What literature can do for children. In Z. Sutherland & M. Livingston (Eds.), *Scott, Foresman anthology of children's literature* (pp. 810–826). Glenview, IL: Scott, Foresman.

Nilsen, A., Peterson, R., & Searfoss, L. (1980). The adult as critic vs. child as reader. *Language Arts, 57,* 530–539.

Oppenheim, J., Brenner, B. & Boegehold, B. O. (1986). *Choosing books for kids.* New York: Ballantine.

Prescott, O. (1965). *A father reads to his children.* New York: Dutton.

Ravitch, D., & Finn, C. (1987). *What do our 17-year-olds know?* New York: Harper & Row.

Roberts, E. E. (1984). *The children's picture book.* Cincinnati: Writer's Digest.

Stewig, J. W. (1980). *Children and literature.* Boston: Houghton Mifflin.

Yawkey, T., & Yawkey, M. (1976). Analysis of picture books. *Language Arts, 53,* 545–548.

Children's Books

Aardema, V. (1975). *Why mosquitoes buzz in people's ears.* New York: Dial.

Andersen, H. C. (1987). *The ugly duckling* (retold by M. Mayer). New York: Macmillan. (Orginally published in 1835)

Asch, F. (1981). *Happy birthday, moon.* Englewood Cliffs, NJ: Prentice-Hall.

Bannerman, H. (1923). *Little Black Sambo.* New York: Lippincott.

de Paola, T. (1981). *The comic adventures of Old Mother Hubbard and her dog.* New York: Harcourt Brace Jovanovich.

Hoberman, M. A. (1979). *A house is a house for me.* New York: Viking.

Rosenberg, M. B. (1983). *My friend Leslie.* New York: Lothrop, Lee & Shepard.

Rylant, C. (1986). *Night in the country.* New York: Bradbury.

Steptoe, J. (1984). *The story of jumping mouse.* New York: Lothrop, Lee & Shepard.

Wells, R. (1975). *Morris's disappearing bag: A Christmas story.* New York: Dial.

Chapter 3

BRINGING PICTURE BOOKS AND YOUNG CHILDREN TOGETHER

*One could talk about literature as a
form of communication, as
expression or as artifact . . .
however, literature is an experience
and, further, an experience not
discontinuous with other
experiences.*

Norman Holland, Five Readers
Reading

What happens when children of various ages are brought together
with favorite books? As Holland (1975) suggests, and as has
been passionately believed by expert teachers, children's librarians,
and teacher educators throughout much of this century, children's
own experience and literature are intertwined. Important learning
takes place, and literature contributes to the child's development (see
Figure 3.1).

In observational studies of preschoolers, Snow and Ninio (1986)
identified the following "contracts of literacy" — basic ideas about literature that young children acquire during adult-child interaction with
picture books. The following examples include some picture books
that are classics and some that are less well regarded but widely
available. Although it is desirable to introduce children to the best
that literature has to offer, it is true that children enjoy and respond
to a wide range of books. How do picture books of various types
teach children the "contracts of literacy"?

Books are for reading, not manipulating. Through experience,
children recognize that a book differs from a toy. They learn that
picture books are "not for eating, throwing, chewing or building
towers" (Snow & Ninio, 1986, p. 122). Children also learn to hold
the book right side up, to begin at the beginning, and to turn the
pages one at a time.

Figure 3.1
Picture Books To Meet the Child's Developmental Needs

Preschoolers' needs	Characteristics of preschoolers	Categories of picture books
active participation	*physically active* — learn through the senses and exploration of the environment	self-help skill books, cloth & board books, novelty books
imagining	*imaginative and playful* — enjoy pretending; take pleasure in identifying ridiculous situations, such as slapstick, role reversals, and incongruous situations	humorous books, fantasy, adventure
self-esteem	*unique* — need a positive self-image and an appreciation of individuality	mood books, books about dealing with powerful emotions, books about children with special needs
secure attachments	*social and affiliative* — need to relate interpersonally and to develop prosocial skills	books about relationships with significant others
knowledge	*expressive and inquisitive* — need to acquire knowledge and classify information	concept books, information books, wordless books
cultural connections	*culturally diverse* — need to appreciate cultural diversity and to begin to understand human motivation	nursery rhymes, books with multicultural concepts, folk tales, fairy tales
mastering and enjoying language	*communicative* — need to explore language, use verbal symbols, and appreciate the rhythm of words	picture story books, song picture books, poetry and stories told in verse

The characteristics of pictures. Children learn that pictures can be labeled and that pictures, "even though static, can represent dynamic actions, events, sequences, relations, motives, and conse-quences" (Snow & Ninio, 1986, p. 132). Pictures are so powerful, at least initially, that children believe the pictures (rather than the words) are being read (Sulzby, 1985).

Listen to Hua, a 30-month-old, discussing *Babies* (Fujikawa, 1963).

*Babies**
(Fujikawa, 1963)

Text of the book	Hua, 30 months old
Babies are very little, soft, warm and cuddly.	Baby! *(She points to the picture of a toddler.)* Tat his big sister.
They are always lying around eating, sleeping, laughing or crying.	Baby lyin' down. Baby eatin'. He's laughin', she's cryin'. Oh, Baby sleepin' with her dolly.
They like to be changed and bathed and hugged and loved.	Baby takin' a tubby. Look, a quack, quack. Mommy huggin' baby, baby wanna story.
Then they eat and go to sleep again.	One, two, three baby, four, five babies. Babies eatin' and sleepin'. He tumblin' on his head.
And how they grow and grow	Baby playin' with kitty. Tat baby playin' ball. This baby crawlin'.
And grow.	He pushin' a car, car.
Before you know it, they will be running and chasing all around,	Babies runnin'. See kitty? Babies chasin' kitty and buderflies.
Oh, so busily . . .	Run little kitty, run away home.
And do lots of things by themselves.	Baby eatin' by herself. Puttin' on her socks. Baby readin' to kitty. Dada proud of baby.
Sometimes they are naughty	Oh! Bad baby. Momma mad.
And sometimes they are little angels.	*(She points to halo.)* Wassat, momma? Baby sittin' with dolly.
But good or bad, all babies like to be hugged and cuddled and loved.	Momma huggin' and kissin' baby. Baby love momma. Momma love baby.

* From *Babies* by Gyo Fujikawa. Copyright © 1963 by Gyo Fujikawa. Reprinted by permission of the publisher, The Putnam & Grosset Group.

The things that Hua chose to mention are a mixture of details observed in the pictures, words heard from the text, discussions from previous story reading sessions, and experience in her own young life. Hua has learned that pictures can do more than represent objects, they can communicate behavior, motivation, and outcomes.

The book is in control, the reader is led. Children learn that the picture book is the focus of the conversation and that a relationship exists between pictured events and real-life events. After young children listen to adults making these connections between life and art, they begin to do so themselves (Snow & Ninio, 1986).

Cars and Trucks and Things That Go*
(Scarry, 1974)

Page	Text of the book	Jamal, 3 years old
1	Tweet! goes the policeman's whistle. All the trucks stop.	Is that the policeman? What is he doing?
2	Here comes the school bus. The children crowd in.	They can't go in there because it's just a page. That's why.
5	The grocery man and his helper carry out packages.	The blue boy with the D on his shirt is helping her?
6, 7	The gasoline truck brings gas to the service station — "fill her up" says the laundry man in his truck.	He's getting gas. Is that a tank truck? It's red.
8	The telephone is broken. Out comes the repair truck.	You mean this line? Does that work? See, those two lines are broken. What happened to them?
10	Here comes a tow truck towing a taxi. See the flat tire!	Who crashed into it? That one has a flat tire. Why? Does it work with a flat tire?
11	Beep! Beep! A police car and a jeep whiz by.	Who's making that noise on there? Why? Our car goes past everyone's cars.
12	The coal truck dumps coal down the chute . . .	Is all that going down? What's that? Spoons? Is that a chute?
14	This family is taking a quiet country vacation . . .	What are they doing? Did he grow up? Did she grow up? What was her name when she was little?
16	Here comes the mail truck to pick up the mail.	He's getting mail. We put cards in there, and the mailman takes them out.
17	A man sells ice cream. A delivery motorcycle hurries by.	Is he an ice cream man? He's delivering his ice cream cones.
18	Look at the big streamlined double decker bus . . .	Did you say a digger? What kind is that truck?
21	What a busy street. See all the cars and trucks hurry by.	Are they going home? Where's the pink one? Where's the flat tire on there?

* From *Cars and Trucks and Things That Go* by Richard Scarry. Copyright © 1974 by Richard Scarry. Used by permission of Western Publishing Company, Inc.

Notice that questions predominate in Jamal's comments. He supplies a few answers as well, noting, for instance, that children cannot really climb into a picture of the schoolbus. He also relates the pictures to his own experiences by remarking that he has mailed cards in a mailbox just like the story characters. Jamal has learned to allow the book to be the focus of conversation.

Events in books are part of a different time frame and world. The young child who experiences stories soon realizes that the discussion of a book takes place in the here and now and that imaginary characters can take on a life of their own. A "child can share a character's attitudes, approve or disapprove of their behavior, and can even exhort them to act differently" (Snow & Ninio, 1986, p. 135).

As children gain experience with literature, their comments about picture books reflect an awareness that stories and characters exist independently of themselves, even though relationships may exist between books and personal experience. In her retelling of Disney's *Lady and the Tramp,* (The Walt Disney Company, 1954), 4-year-old Kiersten stops to comment on an issue she is resolving at home and at child care — where and when she is supposed to sleep. She also begins to talk directly to the main character.

Lady and the Tramp*
(The Walt Disney Company, 1954)

Page	Text of the book	Kiersten, 4 years old
1	One Christmas Eve Jim Dear gave his wife Darling a present. Darling opened the present carefully. Out popped a little puppy . . .	Once there was a man Burt who was married to his wife Darling. He gave Darling a present. It was a very nice one. It was a baby pup. She opened the gift.
3	"Oh, what a lovely puppy!" said Darling. "Let's call her Lady" . . .	He said, "How do you like it Darling?" She said, "I like it very much." "Thank you, honey. I really like it. I really do. Maybe when he grows up he'll know better too". . .
11	At bedtime, Jim tucked Lady into a cozy basket. "That's your very own bed," said Jim.	This is your bed, Lady. It's your bed, Lady. Stay in there, Lady, or else you'll get tireder, so you better sleep in your own bed or Mrs. Sara or Mrs. Reness will get mad at you.

* Exerpts from *Lady and the Tramp,* a Little Golden Book. © 1954 The Walt Disney Company. Used by permission of copyright owner.

Kiersten has learned to regard picture books as part of a fictional world where characters take on a life of their own. She is also learning to interpret the language that she hears and to use "book-like" vocabulary. Later on, the text reads, "But some mean dogs barked at her. Lady ran and ran" (p. 26). Kiersten says, "There were two dogs that dangered her." This use of "dangered" is a good example of applying what she knows about language. Kiersten has heard words like *danger, dangerous,* or perhaps *endangered.* Now she invents a verb to describe the story's meaning.

Eventually, preschoolers begin to tell their favorite story in a way that more closely approximates the text of the book. These retellings often include some verbatim phrases from the story:

The Tale of Peter Rabbit*
(Potter, 1902)

Page	Text of the book	Jonise, 4 years old
9	Once upon a time there were four little Rabbits, and their names were — Flopsy, Mopsy, Cotton-tail, and Peter.	Once 'pon a time there were Flopsy, Mopsy, and Peter Cottontail.
10	'Now, my dears,' said old Mrs. Rabbit one morning, 'you may go into the fields or down the lane, but don't go into Mr. McGregor's garden. . . .'	Mrs. Rabbit said, "Go an' play but don't go to old Mr. Gregor's garden." An' she left.
13	'Now run along, and don't get into mischief. I am going out.'	
14	Then old Mrs. Rabbit took a basket and her umbrella, and went through the woods to the baker's.	Mrs. Rabbit left with her basket to go shoppin'.
17	Flopsy, Mopsy, and Cotton-tail, who were good little bunnies, went down the lane to gather blackberries:	The three good rabbits went to get blackberries for dinner.
18	But Peter, who was very naughty, ran straight away to Mr. McGregor's garden, and squeezed under the gate!	But Peter went to Mr. Gregor's garden under the gate . . .
[After Mr. McGregor chases Peter with a rake:]		
50	Peter got down very quietly off the wheelbarrow, and started running as fast as he could go. . . . He slipped underneath the gate, and was safe at last in the wood outside the garden.	Peter squished under the gate and escaped. (Jonise pronounces this word as "x-scaped.")
53	Mr. McGregor hung up the little jacket and the shoes for a scare-crow to frighten the blackbirds.	The scarecrow wore the jacket an' shoes.
54	Peter never stopped running or looked behind him till he got home to the big fir-tree. He was so tired that he flopped down upon the nice soft sand on the floor of the rabbit-hole and shut his eyes. His mother was busy cooking; she wondered what he had done with his clothes.	Peter got home and flopped down on the floor. Mrs. Rabbit was cookin' when Peter came home an' wondered where his clothes were.

Page	Text of the book	Jonise, 4 years old
56	I am sorry to say that Peter was not very well during the evening. 　　His mother put him to bed and made some camomile tea; and she gave a dose of it to Peter!	Peter's mom made some cammy tea 'cause he didn't feel well.
59	But Flopsy, Mopsy, and Cotton-tail had bread and milk and blackberries for supper.	Flopsy, Mopsy, and Peter Cottontail had a good supper.

* From *The Tale of Peter Rabbit* by Beatrice Potter. Copyright © 1902 by Frederick Warne & Co. Reprinted by permission of the publisher, Penguin Books, Ltd.

Repeated readings of the same story give young children an opportunity not only to bring their experience to the book, but to regard the book itself as an experience. Examples of picture books that have "come alive" for children are illustrated on pages 44 – 45. Returning to the identical text again and again enables children to glimpse the structure of language, to build a foundation for subsequent experiences.

Which Book for Which Child?

Heinrich, a 3-year-old, likes *Where's Spot?* (Hill, 1980) because it is a lift-the-flap book "with a monkey in the cupboard." Bruce, a first grader, appreciates *Goodnight Moon* (Brown, 1947) because "I never read a book where it says good night to everything." Maria, a 4-year-old, likes *The Three Little Kittens* (Cauley, 1982) because "it has a happy ending."

These comments from children relate to three basic ways of describing books: by format, by genre, and by traditional elements.

Format. The physical configuration of a book, such things as a book's size, shape, illustrations, arrangement, and spacing, are all examples of format. In terms of size, a book might be printed in a $3'' \times 5''$ version and also in an $18'' \times 22''$ big book version like *Noisy Nora* (Wells, 1973). Books that are very popular like *The Very Hungry Caterpillar* (Carle, 1969) are sometimes reprinted as pocket-sized books so that children's favorites are more portable. Often the theme of the story affects its format. Not surprisingly, a book called *The Teeny Tiny Woman* (Zemach, 1965) is undersized.

Books for children sometimes have unique characteristics such as pages made of cardboard for toddlers, movable parts, or "pop-up," three-dimensional objects. These are referred to as toy books, participation books, or novelty books.

The Story About Ping (Flack, 1933)

The Polar Express (Van Allsburg, 1985)

Four 5-year-olds' drawings of their favorite story characters.

Mr. Rabbit and the Lovely Present (Zolotow, 1962)

←Sails→

The little cabin of the Maggie B.

The Maggie B (Haas, 1975)

Two books by Ahlberg and Ahlberg emphasize the uniqueness of format. In *Peek-a-Boo!* (1981), a small circle is cut out of every other page. The pictures and the words encourage a young child to describe whatever the baby in the story sees from different vantage points, such as his crib. In *The Jolly Postman and Other People's Letters,* the Ahlbergs (1986) have designed some pages that are letters and envelopes. The envelopes contain imaginative correspondence from one storybook character to another, such as a letter of apology from Goldilocks to the Three Bears. When a child responds enthusiastically to a particular format, teachers might suggest additional books with unique formats such as *The Very Busy Spider* (Carle, 1985) in which children can touch and feel the web as it is being built.

Of course, books can be converted into audiovisual formats as well. In this era of visual media, many excellent picture books for children are becoming available in book/record, book/cassette, film, or video-cassette formats. Many large libraries now have extensive collections of these materials to be loaned free of charge. Appendix D contains a list of high-quality videocassettes based on picture books.

Genre. Another dimension of literature, genre refers to the specific type or category of book. Poetry and prose, nonfiction and fiction are the major genres for picture books. Poetry for young children includes nursery rhymes, picture books based upon song, and stories told in verse such as *Barn Dance!* (Martin, 1987).

Nonfiction prose includes concept books, information books, and biography.

Roberts (1984) has some interesting analogies for children's nonfiction prose. She likens *concept books* to a commercial for an idea. The book "sells" a basic concept like letters, colors, shapes, numbers, or opposites to the child. The alphabet book *Alphabatics* (MacDonald, 1987) is an excellent example of a concept book.

Roberts (1984) regards *information books* as a child's version of an article in *National Geographic* or *Scientific American.* The child has questions about a topic that can be answered by factual information. Children may wonder aloud "Who made this book?" and Aliki's (1986) *How a Book Is Made* gives a clear and accurate explanation. They may want to understand a complex social issue like adoption or be prepared for a routine physical examination. Information books like *Being Adopted* (Rosenberg, 1984) or *A Doctor's Tools* (DeSantis, 1985) answer these questions.

"How to" books also fit into this category. A book that explains how to conduct a simple science experiment or how to make popcorn is a subcategory of the information book.

Information books that tell a true story about an actual person are *biography.* Generally speaking, biography is more appropriate for children in the primary grades or older. One biography suitable for children in the primary grades is *The Man Who Loved Animals* (Hoff,

1982), which tells the story of the founder of the American Society for the Prevention of Cruelty to Animals.

Fictional prose is less dependent upon fact and more dependent upon the writer's imagination. Most picture story books for young children fall into this category. The story characters may be animals who behave like people or people with extraordinary powers. If the book is similar to real-life situations, it is called *realistic fiction*. If it bears little resemblance to objective reality, then the book is categorized as *fantasy*.

Fantasy for young children is found in familiar folk tales such as *The Little Red Hen* (Wilburn, 1984) or modern folk tales like *One Fine Day* (Hogrogian, 1971). Fairy tales are also included in fictional prose.

Traditional elements. Another way to describe and discuss picture books is by the five basic elements of literature. The *traditional elements of literature* are plot, characters, setting, style, and theme or motif.

Several books can share the same basic *plot. The Tale of Peter Rabbit* (Potter, 1902), *The Gingerbread Boy* (Caldone, 1975), *Squawk to the Moon, Little Goose* (Preston & Cooney, 1976), and *A Crocodile's Tale* (Aruego, 1972) are all stories in which a small character is captured by a hungry predator, outwits the villain, and safely returns home.

Picture books might also be categorized by the main *characters*— books about children with imaginary companions or physical handicaps, for example.

Books can share similar *settings. Crictor* (Ungerer, 1958), *Miss Nelson Is Missing* (Allard & Marshall, 1977), and *Next Year I'll Be Special* (Giff, 1980) all have school and classrooms as their primary setting.

A fourth way of classifying literature is by *style.* Two bedtime stories with distinctive styles are *David and Dog* (Hughes, 1977) and the counting book *Ten, Nine, Eight* (Bang, 1983).

Many books also share similar *themes or motifs* (Barton, 1986; Peller, 1962). Some of the most common themes or motifs in picture books are:

Question and Answer —
Questions are posed and answered.
Example: Jesse Bear, What Will You Wear? (Carlstrom, 1986)

Infinity Stories —
The story is circular and ends with the beginning.
Example: Round Trip (Jonas, 1983)

Cumulative Tales —
Each element of the story is repeated as new characters are added.
Example: The Napping House (Wood, 1984)

Chronological Stories —
Time elements such as days of the week, hours of the day, and ordinal numbers are used to organize the story.
Example: The Last Puppy (Asch, 1980)

The Quest —
The main character searches for something, has an adventure, and returns safely home.
Example: Hey, Al (Yorinks, 1986)

Security —
The literature creates a warm and comfortable mood.
Example: Owl Moon (Yolen, 1988)

Role Reversals —
A child (often the smallest character) performs remarkable deeds that surpass even the accomplishments of adults.
Example: Music, Music for Everyone (Williams, 1984)

Any facet of literature, singly or in combination, might explain why a particular child loves a particular book. One of the things that makes the teacher's role difficult is the fact that many excellent books for young children practically defy categorization.

A book like *Watch the Stars Come Out* (Levinson, 1985) is a good example. It relates a young girl's experience as an immigrant to the United States. Although the story is written in prose, it is definitely poetic. Factual information — such as detail about arriving at Ellis Island — is evident, but the book also has a nostalgic quality. One could argue that the book is historical fiction, a story about family relationships, or a metaphor for the immigrant experience. Quality literature is so rich that it can be described in many different ways. Attempts to classify literature are like tasting a delicious food and trying to figure out the recipe. We may be able to say with certainty that it contains particular ingredients, but it is the blending of those components that produces an appealing product. Quite naturally, it is not only *which* book is shared but also *how* it is shared with children that makes a difference.

How To Share a Book With a Young Child

1. *Begin with a quality book.* Use a resource such as the children's book reviews in *Young Children* or "Books for Everychild: Picture Book Classics" (Appendix B) and "Children's Editors' Choices" published by the American Library Association. Make a list of several that sound interesting, based upon the annotated bibliography. Then go to the library.

2. *Review several books.* Begin by locating several of your choices. Skim through each book by looking at the pictures. This is what children will see, so the visual impression is important. If the pictures of a book appeal to you, go back through and read the text. If the text of the book is appealing as well, go back through and read the text and pictures together. Consider how you would present it to children and imagine what their responses are likely to be.

3. *Select a book that you enjoy and one that the children enjoy as well.* Sometimes we assume that the stories we enjoyed as children are the best selections. But many books published before 1970 include stereotypes about women and minorities (Chambers, 1983). There is also the possibility that the books you heard as a child were selected more on the basis of availability than on the basis of quality. Or, your childhood favorites, while excellent, may not be well suited to the developmental level of the children in your group. Even though *Charlotte's Web* (White, 1952) is a children's classic, it is too sophisticated for most preschoolers and many first graders.

4. *Consider the curricular implications.* Look for books like *Wolf's Favor* (Testa, 1986) that are suitable for storytelling and dramatization, seasonal books like *The Polar Express* (Van Allsburg, 1985), and books that tie in with specific content, like *Sophie's Bucket* (Stock, 1985) for a unit on the seashore. Make notes about when and how to share these stories with children. Discuss several of your long-term projects with the librarian and ask for recommendations. There are many resources for teachers that can help you quickly locate stories on a particular topic or theme (Dreyer, 1985; Lima, 1982).

5. *Practice presenting and reading literature aloud.* Consider how you will introduce the book to the children. One teacher showed her preschool class several eggs of different shapes, sizes, and colors before reading *Chickens Aren't the Only Ones* (Heller, 1981). Another teacher used a small toy mouse to introduce *Whose Mouse Are You?* (Kraus, 1970).

When reading aloud to children remember that your voice is an important tool. It can be used to differentiate among characters or to emphasize an important story element. An adult reading *Chicken Little* (Kellogg, 1985) can give Chicken Little a squeaky little voice and make the fox sound sly and gruff.

Sometimes adults who read to children get overly dramatic. A preschooler who heard a particularly chilling rendition of *The Three Billy Goats Gruff* handed the book to her mother and said, "Here, burn this." It *is* possible for adults to get carried away and "perform" a book rather than share it. The human voice can be used far more subtly and effectively. To appreciate how slight those changes might be, try this: Read a sentence while smiling, then read the same sentence with a passive expression on your face. Notice that you can actually hear the smile in your voice. It softens the consonants. Practice reading the book aloud so that your voice is used effectively.

6. *Develop questioning skills.* Although children need to understand that the book is the focus of the conversation, recognize that the child's "agenda" usually differs from an adult's. When the adult-child interaction about a book becomes stilted and predictable, the adult is being too directive. Here is a parent discussing *ABC* (Szekeres, 1983) with 2½-year-old Joshua:

Parent: And what's this over here?

Joshua: It a bunny.

Parent: And what's that?

Joshua: That gwasses.

Parent: Glasses, okay.

Joshua: What eated this?

Parent: What is that?

Joshua: It's a bagel.

Parent: It's a bagel too. Okay.

Notice the child's question, "What eated this?" is ignored. Compare this approach with the following dialogue. George, a 33-month old, is looking at a picture book that shows animals in their home: a kitten in a basket, a bird in a nest, and a frog in a pond.

George: (pointing to the picture of the kitten) Him sleeps on soft pillow. (pointing to the picture of the bird) Birdy.

Parent: Where does the bird sleep?

George: Nest! (imitates bird opening mouth for food)

Parent: Do you eat worms?

George: No! Yuk! Gross! (looking at the picture of the frog) Frog swims on water. Ribbet, ribbet.

Parent: Does George like to swim in the water?

George: I kick, kick, kick. I go swim in baby pool, not big pool.

Here the conversation is focused, but there is room for comments and interaction.

When teachers share stories with groups of children, there is a limit to the amount of discussion that can transpire before a story begins to lose momentum. Expert teachers use professional judgment to decide when the children's attention needs to be redirected to the book. As children acquire additional experience with literature, they will become more skilled at focusing discussions on the story or on personal experience *related* to the story.

Talking about picture books becomes far more pleasurable when adults ask questions without obvious right and wrong answers, questions that challenge children's thinking.

When teachers use open-ended discussion techniques, children have opportunities to talk about literature in more meaningful ways (Hoffman & Knipping, 1988; Paley, 1981). Some recommended questions and comments about picture books are:

What do you think?
Why? Why did . . . ?
What would happen if . . . ?
Tell me more about . . .
Do you mean that . . .
I wonder how . . .
Maybe we act a little bit like _____ when he or she . . .
Did you ever . . . ?

Dialogue about literature need not be children parroting back details recalled from the story. Instead, it can and should be a window on each child's thought process, a means of developing communication skills, and a way for teachers and parents to glimpse children's growth in literacy.

From *The Last Puppy* by Frank Asch. Copyright © 1980 by Frank Asch. Reprinted by permission of the publisher, Prentice-Hall, Inc., Englewood Cliffs, New Jersey.

References

Barton, B. (1986). *Tell me another*. Exeter, NH: Heinemann.

Chambers, B. (1983). Counteracting racism and sexism in children's books. In O. Saracho & B. Spodek (Eds.), *Understanding the multicultural experience in early childhood education* (pp. 91–105). Washington, DC: NAEYC.

Dreyer, S. S. (1985). *The bookfinder* (Vol. 3). Circle Pines, MN: American Guidance Service.

Hoffman, S., & Knipping, N. (1988, April). *Learning through literature*. Paper presented at the Meeting of the Association for Childhood Education International, Salt Lake City, UT.

Holland, N. (1975). *Five readers reading*. New Haven, CT: Yale University Press.

Lima, C. W. (1982). *A to zoo: Subject access to children's picture books*. New York: Bowker.

Paley, V. G. (1981). *Wally's stories*. Cambridge, MA: Harvard University Press.

Peller, L. E. (1962). Daydreams and children's favorite books. In J. F. Rosenblith & W. Allenmith (Eds.), *The causes of behavior: Readings in child development and educational psychology* (pp. 405–411). Boston: Allyn & Bacon.

Roberts, E. E. (1984). *The children's picture book*. Cincinnati: Writer's Digest.

Snow, C., & Ninio, A. (1986). The contracts of literacy: What children learn from learning to read books. In W. Teale & E. Sulzby (Eds.), *Emergent literacy: Writing and reading* (pp. 116–138). Norwood, NJ: Ablex.

Sulzby, E. (1985). Children's emergent reading of favorite storybooks: A developmental study. *Reading Research Quarterly, 20*, 458–481.

Children's Books

Ahlberg, J., & Ahlberg, A. (1981). *Peek-a-boo!* New York: Viking.

Ahlberg, J., & Ahlberg, A. (1986). *The jolly postman and other people's letters*. Boston: Little, Brown.

Aliki. (1986). *How a book is made*. New York: Crowell.

Allard, H., & Marshall, J. (1977). *Miss Nelson is missing*. Boston: Houghton Mifflin.

Aruego, J. (1972). *A crocodile's tale/Cuento de un cocodrilo*. New York: Scholastic.

Asch, F. (1980). *The last puppy*. Englewood Cliffs, NJ: Prentice-Hall.

Bang, M. (1983). *Ten, nine, eight*. New York: Greenwillow.

Brown, M. (1947). *Goodnight moon*. New York: Harper & Row.

Caldone, P. (1975). *The gingerbread boy*. New York: Houghton/Clarion.

Carle, E. (1969). *The very hungry caterpillar*. New York: Philomel.

Carle, E. (1985). *The very busy spider*. New York: Philomel.

Carlstrom, N. (1986). *Jesse Bear, what will you wear?* New York: Macmillan.

Cauley, L. (1982). *The three little kittens*. New York: Putnam.

DeSantis, K. (1985). *A doctor's tools*. New York: Dodd, Mead.

Flack, M. (1933). *The story about Ping*. New York: Viking.

Fujikawa, G. (1963). *Babies*. New York: Putnam.

Giff, P. (1980). *Next year I'll be special*. New York: Dutton.

Haas, I. (1975). *The Maggie B*. New York: Atheneum.

Heller, R. (1981). *Chickens aren't the only ones*. New York: Grosset & Dunlap.

Hill, E. (1980). *Where's Spot?* New York: Putnam.

Hoberman, M. (1978). *A house is a house for me*. New York: Puffin.

Hoff, S. (1982). *The man who loved animals*. New York: Putnam/Coward McCann.

Hogrogian, N. (1971). *One fine day*. New York: Macmillan.

Hughes, S. (1977). *David and dog*. Englewood Cliffs, NJ: Prentice Hall.

Jonas, A. (1983). *Round trip*. New York: Greenwillow.

Kellogg, S. (1985). *Chicken Little*. New York: Morrow.

Kraus, R. (1970). *Whose mouse are you?* New York: Scholastic.

Levinson, R. (1985). *Watch the stars come out*. New York: Dutton.

MacDonald, S. (1987). *Alphabatics*. New York: Bradbury.

Martin, B. (1987). *Barn dance!* New York: Holt, Rinehart & Winston.

Preston, E.M., & Cooney, B. (1976). *Squawk to the moon, little goose*. New York: Penguin.

Potter, B. (1920). *The tale of Peter Rabbit*. Middlesex, England: Warne.

Rosenberg, M. (1984). *Being adopted*. New York: Lothrop, Lee & Shepard.

Scarry, R. (1974). *Cars and trucks and things that go*. New York: Random House.

Stock, C. (1985). *Sophie's bucket*. New York: Lothrop, Lee & Shepard.

Szekeres, C. (1983). *ABC*. New York: Western.

Testa, F. (1986). *Wolf's favor*. New York: Dial.

Ungerer, T. (1958). *Crictor*. New York: Harper & Row.

Van Allsburg, C. (1985). *The polar express*. Boston: Houghton Mifflin.

Walt Disney Company. (1954). *Lady and the Tramp*. (Little Golden Book). New York: Western.

Wells, R. (1973). *Noisy Nora*. New York: Dial.

White, E.B. (1952). *Charlotte's web*. New York: Harper & Row.

Williams, V.B. (1984). *Music, music for everyone*. New York: Greenwillow.

Wilburn, K. (1984). *The little red hen*. New York: Putnam/Grosset.

Wood, A. (1984). *The napping house*. New York: Harcourt Brace Jovanovich.

Yorinks, A. (1986). *Hey, Al*. New York: Farrar, Straus & Giroux.

Yolen, J. (1988). *Owl moon*. New York: Philomel.

Zemach, M. (1965). *The teeny tiny woman*. New York: Scholastic.

Zolotow, C. (1962). *Mr. Rabbit and the lovely present*. New York: Harper & Row.

For Further Reading

Cliatt, M.J.P., & Shaw, J.M. (1988). The storytime exchange: Ways to enhance it. *Childhood Education, 64*(5), 293–298.

Jacobs, L. (1990). Listening to literature. *Teaching K-8, 20*(4), 34–37.

Jalongo, M.R. (1991). *Strategies for developing children's listening skills*. Bloomington, IN: Phi Delta Kappa.

Hickman, J., & Cullinan B.E. (Eds.). *Children's literature in the classroom: Weaving Charlotte's Web*. Needham Heights, MA: Christopher-Gordon.

Smith, C.B. (1989). Reading aloud: An experience for sharing. *The Reading Teacher, 42*(4), 320.

Strickland, D.S., & Morrow, L.M. (1989). Interactive experiences with storybook reading. *The Reading Teacher, 42*(41), 322–323.

Wells, G. (1990). Creating the conditions to encourage literate thinking. *Educational Leadership, 47*, 13–17.

Chapter 4
HOW DO CHILDREN RESPOND TO LITERATURE?

*Today's children are tomorrow's
reading adults. If today's adults
don't care about children's
imaginations or their books, if they
don't sense the strong connection,
children certainly won't. Today's
adults will lose a golden opportunity
for pleasure and tomorrow's adults
may lose the passion for literature
and learning.*

Betsy Hearne, Choosing Books for
Children*

D onald Hall's (1979) book, *Ox-Cart Man,* is a simple story that
chronicles the change of seasons from the perspective of one
person's worklife. The central character is a somber-looking, bearded
farmer. The setting is Colonial America. A person unfamiliar with the
book would probably read this description and decide that young
children would not like it very much. The time, place, and people are
dissimilar to the society in which young children live. And yet, when
the ox-cart man takes the ox he raised from a calf to be sold and
kisses it once on the nose in farewell, many adults and children
"connect" with the pictures and words of this book. So many, in fact,
that this picture book earned one of the most prestigious awards for
illustrations in a picture book, the Caldecott medal.

    Ox-Cart Man effectively communicates to young children an ab-
stract concept like the recurring rhythm of the seasons. On one
occasion when the story was shared with preschoolers, there was a

* From *Choosing Books for Children* by Betsy Hearne. Copyright © 1981 by Betsy
Hearne. Reprinted by permission of the publisher, Delacorte.

satisfied silence from the group. Then a 4-year-old boy remarked softly, "Now it can start all over again" (Jalongo & Renck, 1984).

Imagine for a moment trying to quantify and evaluate this response from young children. In the first place, most formal systems for evaluating literary response rely upon some tangible product. That quiet, reflective mood simply could not be quantified. The child who spontaneously commented upon his own sense of wonder and feelings of pleasure would be overlooked in a study that took the standard approach of tabulating children's book preferences. But important changes in ways of identifying and interpreting children's responses to literature are taking place.

Influences on Literary Responses

Children's responses to literature are much more than the focus of research. Understanding literary response enables early childhood educators to use literature more effectively. Figure 4.1 is an overview of the many variables affecting children's responses to literature.

Figure **4.1**
Variables Affecting Literary Response

Within the child
— age, sex, race, and ethnicity
— socioeconomic status
— interests and experiences
— cognitive-developmental level
— preferences in literature
— disposition toward books and
    reading

Within the book	**Within the environment**
— content	— availability of books
— literary style	— parents and teachers who
— book format	enjoy reading
— illustrative style	— adults who present literature
— quality	effectively
	— peers who recommend books

Note: Based on Favat, 1977; Galda, 1983; Monson, 1985; and Norvell, 1973.

Literary response operates on three dimensions simultaneously: between thinking over what has occurred and anticipating what is yet to come, between detachment from the book and involvement with it, between unconcious drives and conscious desires (Benton, 1979).

How Children Learn To Respond to Literature

Many theorists and researchers now believe that children *construct* meaning from what they read (Rosenblatt, 1978). Although this may not seem like a very surprising idea, it is. The previous assumption was that the text of a book *had* a meaning and that there were simply more or less accurate readings of the words. From this view, the young child's literary response was usually seen as inferior to that of older children or adults. Now the perspective has changed so that meaning is regarded as a "transaction" between the reader and the book (Rosenblatt, 1978; 1982). The nature of that transaction is greatly affected by the experience a listener or reader brings to the book.

By studying the "reading-like" behavior of emergent readers, like Scot (page 60), we can begin to see how meaning is constructed from print. Notice how Scot's familiarity with the book has enabled him to "absorb" the basic story structure (Meek, 1982) and give an animated rendition of the book.

Marvin K. Mooney, Will You Please Go Now!*
(Dr. Seuss, 1972)

Page	Text of the book	Scot, 3½ years old
2	The time has come. The time is now.	It is time now!
4	Just go . . . Go. Go! I don't care how.	GO! GO! GO! GO! I don't care. GO! GO!
5	You can go by foot. You can go by cow. Marvin K. Mooney, will you please go now!	Go by foot. Go by cow. Marbin K., GO!
6	You can go on skates. You can go on skis.	GO by skateys or go . . . go . . . use skis.
7	You can go in a hat. But please go. Please!	Go in a hat. A HAT that's silly!! GO! PLEASE GO!!!
13	You can go in a Clunk-Car if you wish.	Go in a clunk car.
15	Or stamp yourself and go by mail. Marvin K. Mooney! Don't you know the time has come to go, Go, GO!	Go in the mailman, Marbin K. K. Time to go, GO! GO!!
17	Get on your way! Please, Marvin K.! You might like going in a Zumble-Zay.	Go, Marbin K.! Go in a Bumbley Way!
18	You can go by balloon . . . or by broomstick . . . OR you can go by camel in a bureau drawer.	You can go by bullon or boomstick like witches!
20	Get yourself a Ga-Zoom. You can go with a . . . . BOOM! Marvin, Marvin, Marvin! Will you leave this room!	Go with a BOOM BOOM! Marbin, Marbin, get outa da room!
21	Marvin K. Mooney! Will you please GO NOW!	Marbin K., GO NOW, GO NOW! GO! GO! GO!
22	I said GO and GO I meant . . .	I said GO, GO, GO!!
23	The time had come. So Marvin went.	Time came so Marbin left! THE END!

Adults can easily grow weary of reading the same book over and over again. But observational research with parents and young children sharing favorite books reveals that children use imitation, questions, and comments to construct meaning (Doake, 1985; Snow, 1983; Wells, 1986). By keeping the material constant (experiencing the same book repeatedly), children build a foundation and keep adding additional pieces until an intricate network of ideas and their relationships is produced (Rand, 1984; Rumelhart, 1980). So a child might hear a book about starting school such as *My First Days of School* (Hamilton-Merritt, 1982) and emerge from those repeated readings with a much more sophisticated concept of facts and feelings about initial classroom experiences.

Recent research on the hemispheres of the brain suggests that the left side of the brain is responsible for rational analysis — vocabulary building and labeling, for example. The brain's right side is thought to be responsible for more holistic perception — such as pictorial or visual literacy. Picture books are an ideal learning experience because they stimulate both types of thought simultaneously.

Additionally, young children can deliberately alter their purposes for experiencing the same text. Sometimes they might be listening primarily to obtain information. At other times they might be looking and listening primarily to enjoy the beauty of the art and language. Figure 4.2 is an example using the familiar tale *The Gingerbread Boy* (Cook, 1987; Galdone, 1975) to show how visual literacy and reading comprehension skills are developed and interrelated.

Figure **4.2**
Picture Books, Visual Literacy, and Reading Comprehension

Example using *The Gingerbread Boy* (Cook, 1987; Galdone, 1975)

Visual literacy (Lacy, 1986)	*Child's comments*	*Reading comprehension* (Sutherland, Monson, & Arbuthnot, 1981)
comprehension of the main idea the ability to understand the intended message of the visual work	"Here's the page where he comes alive." "He gets away from all the people and the animals — except the fox."	*literal recall* recall of main idea, sequence, cause-effect, character traits, and details
part/whole relationship the ability to perceive details that contribute to the whole	"Look, he has raisins for his eyes."	*inference* making inferences, predicting outcomes, understanding figurative language
differentiation of fantasy/reality the ability to infer relationships between symbols and reality	"A gingerbread boy can't really run but he does in the story."	*evaluation* judgments of reality/fantasy, fact/opinion, acceptability, and worth
recognition of artistic medium the ability to identify unique properties of the medium used	"Somebody drew these pictures and painted them, maybe." "I like the part where he says, 'Run, run fast as you can. You can't catch me, I'm the Gingerbread Man!'"	*appreciation* reader's/listener's emotional response to the author's plot, theme, characters, and use of language

Observing Young Children's Responses to Literature

It is important for adults to know if children are responding favorably to a particular book. Following are some behaviors to watch for.

Physical

Young children are action-oriented, so their enjoyment of books is often expressed in a concrete way. They will position themselves in close physical proximity to the book, pore over illustrations, hug the book like a treasured toy, or move closer to the reader. During a successful group story session, young children will often start out in a neat semicircle and conclude clustered tightly around the reader's chair. A group of young children who heard *The Quicksand Book* (de Paola, 1977) rushed up to the teacher afterward clamoring to be the first to borrow the book — it just happens to contain a recipe for making quicksand!

Attentional

When reading a book to a child or a group of children, you can easily identify their look of rapt attention. They lean forward with a transfixed facial expression and will protest if the pages are turned too quickly or if they cannot see the book well. They will also chime in at the appropriate moment if a book is predictable or repetitive. Sometimes the children's nonverbal responses will show that they are really listening, understanding a story, and being caught up in it.

Preschoolers who heard *Hazel's Amazing Mother* (Wells, 1985) reacted in this way. When Hazel is tormented by a gang of bullies who tear apart her favorite doll, the children were outraged and audibly gasped. Later, when Hazel's mother frightens the bullies so much that they "quivered like Jello" and "sewed like a machine" to repair Hazel's doll, the preschoolers laughed delightedly and breathed a sign of relief. They were engrossed in the story, and their attention to the details of the story reflected their involvement.

Verbal

Young children often let adults know that they enjoy a story through their words (Zack, 1983). On first hearing *Harry the Dirty Dog* (Zion, 1956), Jarrod asked why everyone in the family fails to recognize their own dog. Then, at a subsequent story session, he commented, "They don't know it's Harry 'cause he's all dirty, right?" Sometime later he remarked, "I don't like this part where nobody knows him."

Another verbal behavior that reflects children's appreciation is the incorporation of storybook language into their vocabulary and play. After Amy heard *Gregory the Terrible Eater* (Sharmat, 1980) several times, she used an expression and a gesture from the book while playing house. When a boy who was pretending to be Amy's offspring misbehaved, she slammed her hand down on the table and said "That does it!" just like Gregory's father in the story.

From *Hazel's Amazing Mother* by Rosemary Wells. Copyright © 1985 by Rosemary Wells. Reprinted by permission of the publisher, Dial Books for Young Readers.

Children often respond to their favorite stories through art, drama, stories, and creative movement. Several examples of young children's writings and drawings in response to literature are on pages 64–66.

A 6-year-old responds to Steven Kellogg's (1985) version of *Chicken Little*.

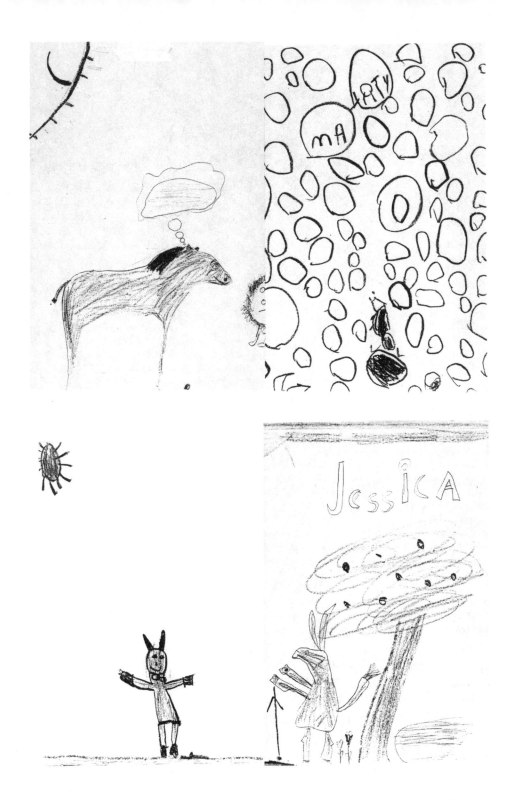

Four first graders illustrate their favorite part of *Sylvester and the Magic Pebble* (Steig, 1969).

Richard, a 5-year-old, draws Clifford the big red dog (Bridwell, 1972). The original was on 18″ × 22″ paper.

The Child as Critic

Canaan, a 5-year-old, thinks that *Some of Us Walk, Some Fly, Some Swim* (Frith, 1971) "was very boring at the beginning . . . because it just keeps telling you the names of things, different animals." But the book "has a real happy ending. Since the fish were halfway dead, all of the birds and the other animals helped the fish and they put them in the water."

Melissa, a first grader, feels *A Children's Zoo* (Hoban, 1985) could be improved: "I would put different words in it, and I'd put in more *baby* animals too."

Corey enjoyed *The Claypot Boy* (Jameson, 1973) "'cause he ate people." But there was something about the plot that bothered him. In the story, the Claypot Boy devours people until a billy goat offers to be the Claypot Boy's dinner and batters his way out, breaking the clay into bits and allowing the people to escape. Corey reasons that volunteering to be eaten is foolhardy: "Instead of saying 'I'll stand here and jump into your mouth,' I would say 'Okay, come over and try to get me . . . and I would bust him just by runnin' into him because it sounds dumb that he is gonna help him eatin' him."

As these evaluative comments from young children illustrate, their responses to literature can be quite insightful. Perhaps young children's responses to literature are more sophisticated than we realize, and it is vocabulary rather than judgment that they lack. At the very least, children have definite preferences and ways of expressing those preferences.

Sources of Picture Book Appeal

Children's books should be a treat for the senses, the mind, and the emotions.

Sensory appeal. Turn the beautifully illustrated pages of *Pumpkin Pumpkin* (Titherington, 1986), and the visual and tactile stimulation is satisfying. Each page is alive with images and the paper feels good against your fingertips. Even the senses not directly affected by the book can be evoked. A listener imagines the smell of the earth as the seed is planted and the taste of salted toasted pumpkin seeds. When a beautifully written story is read, the rhythm of language brings pleasure through the sense of hearing, too.

Intellectual stimulation. Young children are inquisitive. They want to understand themselves and others; they wonder about other people, places, and times. Picture books enable children to ask questions, to obtain answers, and to explore other possibilities. *Mufaro's Beautiful Daughters: An African Folk Tale* (Steptoe, 1987) is a good example. This book instantly transports the listener to another continent that is lush, green, and magical. The characters are clothed in traditional African dress and children immediately notice that the king, prince, and two princesses in this setting are distinctly different from most other portrayals of royalty. The book also stimulates children's imaginations by presenting a prince who can transform himself into a harmless garden snake or an old lady, all in the interest of learning more about the true personality of his future bride. Even the conclusion of the story stimulates the child's mind because the wicked sister's prophecy that her sister will become a servant in her house does not come true. Just the reverse happens and goodness is rewarded. Young children take notice that the roles predicted at the story's beginning have been reversed at the story's conclusion.

Affective appeal. The picture books that children love evoke emotional responses as well. The ridiculous situations in *Animals Should Definitely Not Wear Clothing* (Barrett & Barrett, 1970), such as a porcupine in a perforated shirtwaist, bring smiles and perhaps laughter. Books that deal with childhood crisis issues can be an important way of reassuring children that they are not alone in experiencing such feelings (Jalongo, 1986). *Timothy Goes to School* (Wells, 1981) is a fine example. Rather than presenting the stereotypic story about starting school—all fun and instant friendship, Wells deftly portrays the understandable anxiety about doing something for the first time, functioning as a member of a group, and contending with a know-it-all classmate.

Responses to literature involve feelings, ideas, and sensory perception. How might this knowledge about children's responses to literature be used to improve adults' use of picture books with young children?

Predicting How Children Will Respond

When an adult pulls a picture book from the library shelf and decides to share the story with young children, it would be helpful to *anticipate* children's responses. The ability to predict which books children will prefer would make the whole process much more efficient. There are three basic strategies for making these predictions.

The first involves identifying the developmental issues facing the child. In order to illustrate how this might work, consider some of the issues facing a baby: waiting for a parent to return, being reprimanded for making a mess. These ideas are presented in two board books by Jan Omerod (1985): *Dad's Back* and *Messy Baby*.

A second technique for increasing the likelihood of a favorable response is to base a current selection on past preferences of a child or small group of children. If a humorous story *Bea and Mr. Jones* (Schwartz, 1982), where an advertising executive and a kindergartner trade places, was well received, adults might try another amusing role reversal such as *Swamp Monsters* (Christian, 1983).

The third basic strategy in predicting picture book preferences is to know many excellent books very well. Then you can compare an unfamiliar picture book with others of its type and make equally appropriate choices in the future.

Implications for Practice

Theory and research on literary response has been in existence at least since the first training course in the world for children's librarians was taught in Pittsburgh in 1900 (Meigs, Eaton, Nesbitt, & Viguers, 1969). Research points to the need for more effective teaching practices:

- Because young children rely upon adults for experiences with quality literature, classrooms should be places where many different types of books are accessible to children, shared with children, and recommended to parents and children.

- Because the opportunity to share literature on a one-to-one basis with adults is fundamental to the development of children's literacy, children who come to school without such experiences must obtain them. Educators will need to explore ways of providing young children with individual storytime through community volunteers, college students in education, cross-age tutoring, and parent education programs.

From *Mufaro's Beautiful Daughters* by John Steptoe. Copyright © 1987 by John Steptoe. Reprinted by permission of Lothrop, Lee & Shepard Books (A division of William Morrow & Company, Inc.).

- Because children can respond to literature in many ways, teachers should model a range of responses—verbal, artistic, physical. Children need authentic opportunities for self-expression and creative thought.

- Because previous experiences exert a great influence on literary response, teachers should be deliberate in connecting reading with experience. When children visit a farm, display books about farms. When children connect with a particular theme or format, make additional stories with that theme or format available.

- Because young children are in the process of forming literary preferences, the opportunity to choose from among many books is important. Teachers should introduce a wide variety of book types including fiction and nonfiction, traditional and innovative. Children should also have the experience of comparing/contrasting different versions of the same story.

When parents and teachers consider the child's responses to literature and fulfill these roles, they create an environment in which love of literature and growth in literacy can flourish.

References

Benton, M. (1979). Children's responses to stories. *Children's Literature in Education, 10,* 68–85.

Doake, D. (1985). Reading-like behavior: Its role in learning to read. In M. Jogger & T. Smith-Burke (Eds.), *Observing the language learner* (pp. 82–98). Newark, DE: International Reading Association.

Favat, F. A. (1977). *Child and tale.* Urbana, IL: National Council of Teachers of English.

Galda, L. (1983). Research in response to literature. *Journal of Research and Development in Education, 16*(3), 1–7.

Jalongo, M. R. (1986). Using crisis-oriented books with young children. In J. B. McCracken (Ed.), *Reducing stress in young children's lives* (pp. 41–46). Washington, DC: NAEYC.

Jalongo, M. R., & Renck, M. A. (1984). Looking homeward: Nostalgia in children's literature. *School Library Journal, 31,* 36–39.

Lacy, L. E. (1986). *Art and design in children's picture books.* Chicago: American Library Association.

Meek, M. (Ed.). (1982). *The cool web: The patterning of children's reading.* London: Bodley Head.

Meigs, C., Eaton, A. B., Nesbitt, E., & Viguers, R. H. (1969). *A critical history of children's literature* (rev. ed.). New York: Macmillan.

Monson, D. L. (1985). *Adventuring with books: A booklist for pre-K – grade 6.* Urbana, IL: National Council of Teachers of English.

Norvell, G. W. (1973). *The reading interests of young people.* East Lansing, MI: Michigan State University Press.

Rand, M. K. (1984). Story schema: Theory, research and practice. *Reading Teacher, 37,* 377–382.

Rosenblatt, L. M. (1978). *The reader, the text, the poem: The transactional theory of the literary work.* Carbondale, IL: Southern Illinois University Press.

Rosenblatt, L. M. (1982). The literacy transaction: Evocation and response. *Theory Into Practice, 21,* 268–277.

Rumelhart, D. E. (1980). Schemata: The building blocks of cognition. In R. J. Spiro, B. C. Borce, & W. F. Brewer (Eds.), *Theoretical issues in reading comprehension* (pp. 33–57). Hillsdale, NJ: Erlbaum.

Snow, C. (1983). Literacy and language: Relationships during the preschool years. *Harvard Educational Review, 53,* 165–189.

Sutherland, Z., Monson, D. L., & Arbuthnot, M. H. (1981). *Children and books* (6th ed.). Glenview, IL: Scott, Foresman.

Wells, G. (1986). *The meaning makers: Children learning language and using language to learn.* Portsmouth, NH: Heinemann.

Zack, V. (1983). The parent — the preschool child (0–3) — the book: Ring around the joyful telling. *The Advocate, 86,* 86–94.

Children's Books

Barrett, J., & Barrett, R. (1970). *Animals should definitely not wear clothing.* New York: Putnam.

Bridwell, N. (1972). *Clifford, the small red puppy.* New York: Scholastic.

Christian, M. B. (1983). *Swamp monsters.* New York: Dial.

Cook, S. (1987). *The gingerbread boy.* New York: Knopf.

de Paola, T. (1977). *The quicksand book.* New York: Holiday House.

Frith, M. K. (1971). *Some of us walk, some fly, some swim.* New York: Beginner Books.

Galdone, P. (1975). *The gingerbread boy*. New York: Clarion.

Hall, D. (1979). *Ox-cart man*. New York: Viking.

Hamilton-Merritt, J. (1982). *My first days of school*. New York: Messner.

Hoban, T. (1985). *A children's zoo*. New York: Greenwillow.

Jameson, C. (1973). *The claypot boy*. London: World's Work/McCann & Geoghegan.

Kellogg, S. (1985). *Chicken Little*. New York: Morrow.

Omerod, J. (1985). *Dad's back*. New York: Lothrop, Lee & Shepard.

Omerod, J. (1985). *Messy baby*. New York: Lothrop, Lee & Shepard.

Schwartz, A. (1982). *Bea and Mr. Jones*. New York: Bradbury.

Seuss, Dr. (1972). *Marvin K. Mooney, will you please go now!* New York: Random House.

Sharmat, M. (1980). *Gregory the terrible eater*. New York: Scholastic.

Steig, W. (1969). *Sylvester and the magic pebble*. New York: Scholastic.

Steptoe, J. (1987). *Mufaro's beautiful daughters: An African folk tale*. New York: Lothrop, Lee & Shepard.

Titherington, J. (1986). *Pumpkin pumpkin*. New York: Greenwillow.

Wells, R. (1981). *Timothy goes to school*. New York: Dial.

Wells, R. (1985). *Hazel's amazing mother*. New York: Dial.

Zion, G. (1956). *Harry the dirty dog*. New York: Harper & Row.

More Children's Books

Alborough, J. (1992). *Where's my teddy?* Cambridge, MA: Candlewick.

Beil, K.M. (1992). *Grandma according to me*. New York: Doubleday.

Bottner, B. (1992). *Bootsie Barker bites*. New York: Putnam.

Bradman, T. (1992). *Billy and the baby*. New York: Barron's.

Brown, C.M. (1992). *City sounds*. New York: Greenwillow.

Carlstrom, N. (1992). *How do you say it today, Jesse Bear?* New York: Maxwell Macmillan.

Charbonnet, G. (1992). *Boodil, my dog*. New York: Holt.

Craig, H. (1992). *The town mouse and the country mouse*. Cambridge, MA: Candlewick.

Dalton, A. (1992). *This is the way*. New York: Scholastic.

Falwell, C. (1992). *Shape space*. New York: Clarion.

Gantschev, I. (1991). *Good morning, good night*. Saxonville, MA: Picture Book Studio.

Levinson, R. (1992). *Country dawn to dusk*. New York: Dutton.

Linden, A.M. (1992). *One smiling grandma: A Carribean counting book*. New York: Dial.

Meddaugh, S. (1991). *Martha speaks*. Boston: Houghton Mifflin.

Medearis, A.S. (1992). *Picking peas for a penny*. Austin, TX: State House Press.

Mora, P. (1992). *A birthday basket for Tia*. New York: Maxwell Macmillan.

Shaw, N. (1992). *Sheep out to eat*. Boston: Houghton Mifflin.

Smalls, H. (1992). *Jonathan and his mommy*. Boston: Little, Brown.

Sneed, B. (1992). *Lucky Russell*. New York: Putnam.

Spier, P. (1992). *Peter Spier's Circus!* New York: Doubleday.

Stanley, D. (1992). *Moe the dog in tropical paradise*. New York: Putnam.

Van Laan, N. (1992). *This is the hat: A story in rhyme*. Boston: Joy Street Books.

Watson, J. (1992). *We're the noisy dinosaurs! (crash, bang, wallop)*. Cambridge, MA: Candlewick.

Yee, W.H. (1992). *Eek! There's a mouse in the house*. Boston: Houghton Mifflin.

Chapter 5
PARENTS, CHILDREN, AND PICTURE BOOKS

Just when you think that there isn't enough time for the night's reading, remind yourself how short is your daughter's childhood. I promise you that twenty years from now your television set will still be there . . . but I can also guarantee that twenty years from now your daughter will no longer be your little girl . . .

Jim Trelease, The Read-Aloud Handbook*

A few years ago, several college faculty members conducted a workshop for the parents of kindergartners at a large school district. A reading professor gave the opening speech. During his address to more than 400 parents, he read aloud Judith Viorst's (1971) *The Tenth Good Thing About Barney.* In the story, a boy mourns the death of his cat named Barney. The boy's mother tries to comfort him and suggests that he make a list of ten good things about the pet to read at Barney's funeral.

The college professor had three reasons for reading the book to this group of parents: to demonstrate how to share a book with a child, to show that there is children's literature that is far superior to what is found in grocery and discount stores, and to show that picture books can deal deftly with very serious topics — like the death of a pet. As the parents walked down the hall afterwards to attend small group sessions, one father remarked, "Well, I hope we aren't going to

* From *The Read-Aloud Handbook* by Jim Trelease. Copyright © 1979, 1982, 1985 by Jim Trelease. All rights reserved. Reprinted by permission of Viking Penguin Inc.

sit and listen to any more cute little books. All I want to know is how to make my kid read as soon as possible."

This parent's need to be convinced may be healthy, but the search for easy answers is not. Limiting the answers to those things that are expedient — a kit to buy, a new software program for the computer, the child's enrollment in a Saturday class — increases the likelihood of making errors in judgment. When a thing is difficult or complex, there is always the danger that we may overlook the obvious in search of the obscure.

Parents are sometimes disappointed to hear professionals say that taking the time to read to children is the best way to help children become readers. That answer seems too simple, too commonplace. But parents who go seeking some quick-fix, high-tech solutions are likely not only to waste their money but also to fail in helping their children become avid readers.

Reading aloud to children is more than good, old-fashioned advice. The recommendation is well researched and carefully documented (Clay, 1982; Cochran-Smith, 1984; Teale, 1978).

Reading Aloud and Learning To Read

A recent review of the research literature on parent involvement and reading achievement (Silvern, 1985) noted that reading to children increases their

reading achievement scores

listening and speaking abilities

letter and symbol recognition

ability to use more complex sentences

literal and inferential comprehension skills

concept development

positive attitudes toward reading

tendency to view reading as a valued activity

Durkin's (1966) now classic study, *Children Who Read Early,* was an effort to identify variables that could explain early reading. She found that children who started to read independently during the preschool years were not necessarily gifted. The things that differentiated these young children from their peers were hearing favorite stories; getting answers to questions from at least one literate adult; and an interest in books, words, and letters. These children also observed other family members reading and writing to each other. Unfortunately, many people interpreted Durkin's findings as "proof" that children should memorize the alphabet during toddlerhood. In fact, her research implied just the opposite. The child's love of books *precedes* an interest in learning to read.

What do children need in order to be sold on the idea of learning to read? Martin and Brogan (1972) say that the emerging reader needs many favorite books to zoom through with joyous familiarity. Knowledge and enjoyment of numerous picture books come from sharing literature with caring adults — especially parents (Taylor, 1983). The connection between reading aloud to young children and their eventual success as independent readers is strong and positive (Ferreiro & Teberosky, 1982; Kontos, 1986). Figure 5.1 describes the three basic skill areas fundamental to success in reading and explains how these skills are developed through reading aloud. The comments that children make during story sessions are one of the most useful indicators of the child's growth in literacy.

Figure 5.1
Emergent Reading Abilities: How Reading Aloud Helps

1. Attends to visual cues

Reading abilities	How reading aloud helps	Typical comments from child
The child turns pages of the book correctly; knows that books are read from left to right; has a concept of units of language (words, letters) and matching spoken words to printed ones; recognizes some words in the book.	Children have ample experience with book handling. Opportunities to hear the same story again and again enable them to get a sense of how a book "works."	"Let me hold it. I know how to turn the pages." "Is this where it says his name?" "Here comes the picture where he's wearing his hat." "Where does it say 'and that was that'?"

2. Uses intuitive knowledge of language/expects meaning from print

Reading abilities	How reading aloud helps	Typical comments from child
The child can tell or invent a story based upon illustrations; can relate the basic story from memory (including some exact book passages); learns to expect a story from print.	Children acquire a "sense of story" and understand that it has a beginning, a middle, and a conclusion.	"Watch me read this book." "And it was *just* right." "I can read the newspaper too. Here, I'll read it to you."

3. Begins integration of visual and language cues

Reading abilities	How reading aloud helps	Typical comments from child
The child begins to read single sentences word by word. Knowledge of word order, some beginning sounds, the context, and the predictability of the story are used to read and to tell if an error has been made.	Children often use repetitive books or books based on rhymes and songs they know to emulate reading adults.	"No! You're not reading it right. You forgot the part about the little old man." "This says 'Curious George,' right?" "This starts with 's' but it can't say her name — her name has a big 'S'."

Note: Based on Clay (1979) and McDonnell & Osborn (1978).

Is Earlier Necessarily Better?

The media often publicize cases in which a toddler is taught a few sight words using flash cards or a 3-year-old learns the alphabet. These behaviors seem so precocious that many well-intentioned parents hope to see their child do likewise. After all, this is proof that the child is brilliant and can read, right? Well, not quite. We have all seen trained animals who appear to be able to count. We watch them perform, confident that the animal is completely reliant upon his trainer and really could not use this ability in any meaningful way. Parroting back words and identifying letters at an unusually young age should not impress us all that much.

Although it is true that some children actually learn to read remarkably early, the majority begin with "whole language" (books) rather than bits of language (words and letters). What adults have disparagingly called memorizing a favorite story is actually a greater accomplishment, intellectually speaking, than the highly touted recognition of a few words or letters (Doake, 1985). Children who begin with books approach the task of learning to read as appreciative listeners; they sense the value of being able to read. Children who are conditioned to identify words and letters approach the task of learning to read as a mystifying exercise that somehow pleases adults; they are entirely dependent upon others for motivation. Furthermore, the child who begins doing schoolwork early will not necessarily do any better in school.

An analogy in terms of physical growth is very useful here. What would happen if we pushed a child into riding a bicycle when she had barely learned to ride a tricycle? There are several possibilities. The child would probably be overwhelmed by the demands of the task, fail, and be discouraged — even injured. She could succeed at the task, but a child who had been pressured to learn to ride a bicycle would do it no better (and would probably like it less) than a peer who pursued the task without excessive pressure from adults.

Inappropriate acceleration, whether of physical skills or of academic learning, creates problems. Young children who are pushed into doing mounds of workbook pages and dittos show signs of stress. If they learn the three Rs, they often learn to dislike them. If they have difficulty with academic subjects, they learn to doubt their competence not only in the three Rs, but in general. Children have no way of knowing when adults' expectations for them are inappropriate. When a child cannot master a task at parents' and/or teachers' requests, that child experiences failure.

What, then, is the recommended alternative? The preschool years are a crucial time for the development of language and literacy. Extensive observational research with young children and their families supports a more "natural" approach to early literacy (Jewell & Zintz, 1986; Tovey, Johnson, & Szporer, 1986; Willert & Kamii, 1985).

What is a natural method? If you interviewed the parents of these children, they would say things like: "I never really *taught* Leon how to read; we just kept lots of books around and read together and talked about them. Then we started to make books with family snapshots, and he dictated the captions. Pretty soon he was asking things like 'Where does it say my name?' If I wrote a grocery list or a thank you note, he wanted to write too. And gradually he just started reading and writing." This natural approach to early literacy, often called the language experience method, was used in Progressive schools across the country until recent decades when "reading programs" and workbooks were permitted to squeeze it out. Experiences, discussions, writing about experiences, creative writing, and good literature — these were the ingredients of early literacy programs in many schools for many years (Lee & Allen, 1941).

Evidently, listening to stories is the ideal introduction into the world of books and reading (Fields, 1987).

What Children Learn From Listening to Stories

One reason that many people are skeptical of the value of reading aloud is because it seems that the adult is doing all of the work. But listening, especially where the young language learner is concerned, is much more than hearing the words. "Far from being passive, the listener is extremely busy participating in the recreation of that story: for a successful listener needs to be a storyteller too" (Barton, 1986, p. 9).

Many theorists and researchers have emphasized how important it is for a child to develop a "sense of story" (Applebee, 1978; Favat, 1977; Jacobs, 1965; Snow, 1983).

Three-year-old Melanie illustrates how a sense of story is acquired as she retells the familiar story *Where the Wild Things Are* (Sendak, 1964):

> That night he wears his wolf suit and made mischief of one kind. He be sent to his room with no food. That night the forest grew in his room and grew and grew and GREW! And there went an ocean tumbled down. And there was a private boat for Max. And in and out of weeks to where the wild things are.
>
> They roared their terrible teeth. And gnashed their terrible teeth. "Be still." He did a magic trick without blinking into his eyes. (I heard this before that's why I know all of this.) He was the King of all and said, "Let the wild rumpus start!" He sent them to bed without any supper. (They don't have anything to eat because giraffes just eat leaves.)
>
> He smelled food. He went home in a boat. Into his own bedroom alone where his supper was still hot.

Melanie already knows how a book "works." She understands elements of stories such as characters, action, sequence, and story-book language. She realizes that print is the spoken word written down and that practice with a book will make a person a more proficient reader. Most importantly, she is motivated to read and enjoys trying. Her abilities are a good answer for that impatient father described at the beginning of this chapter. Reading is a complex process involving many subskills. They are learned best when they are learned gradually after years of accumulated experience; they are exceedingly difficult when rushed or forced.

How To Share Picture Books With Your Child

A high school English teacher announced to a group of seniors that she was about to teach them the most important thing they would learn about literature all year. What she taught the students was how to read a book to a child. Reading to children *is* that important. Here are some general guidelines for sharing picture books effectively:

Choosing the book. If you have limited experience with children's books, consult some parent resources such as *For Reading Out Loud!* (Kimmel & Segel, 1984), *The Read-Aloud Handbook* (Trelease, 1985), or *Children's Reading Begins at Home* (Larrick, 1980). Libraries often have recommended reading lists free for the asking. Page 79 shows an example of the type of free material your public library might provide. These were distributed as bookmarks for parents and children to use. Choose several books that you enjoy and that you

STORYBOOK FRIENDS

(all are located in the JE section)

MISS NELSON
Harry Allard

MADELINE
Ludwig Bemelmans

THE BERENSTAIN BEARS
Stan & Jan Berenstain

CLIFFORD, THE BIG RED DOG
Norman Bridwell

ARTHUR
Marc Brown

BABAR THE ELEPHANT
Jean de Brunhoff

EVERETT ANDERSON
Lucille Clifton

DORRIE THE WITCH
Patricia Coombs

THE CAT IN THE HAT
Theodore Geisel

FRANCES THE BADGER
Russell Hoban

FROG AND TOAD
Arnold Lobel

GEORGE & MARTHA
James Marshall

AMELIA BEDELIA
Peggy Parish

PETER RABBIT
Beatrix Potter

CURIOUS GEORGE
H. A. Rey

NATE THE GREAT
Marjorie Sharmat

HARRY THE DIRTY DOG
Gene Zion

TOLEDO-LUCAS COUNTY PUBLIC LIBRARY

21 FOR 1ST & 2ND GRADERS

MORE UNIDENTIFIED FLYING RIDDLES
Joanne Bernstein   j818.5402

GO WEST, SWAMP MONSTERS!
Mary Christian   JE

THE ANSWER BOOK ABOUT ANIMALS
Mary Elting   j591

ARTHUR'S LOOSE TOOTH
Lillian Hoban   JE

WILL YOU CROSS ME?
Marilyn Kaye   JE

WELCOME HOME, BIG BIRD
Emily Kingsley   JE

LIONEL-AT-LARGE
Stephen Krensky   JE

LOOSE TOOTH
Steven Kroll   JE

KATIE COULDN'T
Becky McDaniel   JE

BLACKBERRY INK
Eve Merriam   j811.54

BLACK KITTEN
Eileen Ryder   JE

EAT YOUR PEAS, LOUISE!
Pegeen Snow   JE

A DOZEN DOGS
Harriet Ziefert   JE

OTHER AUTHORS TO TRY

Bonsall, Crosby	*Parish, Peggy*
Hoff, Syd	*Sharmat, Marjorie*
Kessler, Leonard	*VanLeeuwen, Jean*
Lobel, Arnold	*Wiseman, Bernard*
Marshall, Edward	

TOLEDO-LUCAS COUNTY PUBLIC LIBRARY

---

think your child will enjoy, too (see Figure 5.2). If the book does not "grab" you after you look at the pictures and read the text, simply go on to the next until you find several you like.

Figure 5.2
Selecting Books for the Very Young Child

Books for infants, toddlers, and 3-year-olds should:

1. *Contain appropriate themes or subject matter.*
Issues facing the youngest child such as building a sense of trust and expressing autonomy (Erikson, 1963) are examples of general themes that have appeal for young children.

2. *Use language effectively and imaginatively.*
The words in picture books should be precise, eloquent, creative, and evocative. The text of the story should deftly set the scene and move the action along (Butler, 1975).

3. *Include straightforward plots.*
Not all books for the very young are storybooks, but when a story is written for the very young, it should be direct and avoid tangents. *Rosie's Walk* (Hutchins, 1971), in which an unsuspecting hen is followed by a hungry fox, is a good example of a clear, simple plot.

4. *Build to a satisfying conclusion.*
A quality picture storybook comes to a swift resolution and ends on a positive note. The fact that the story has ended should be apparent, even to a child who is just learning how a book "works." The book should have "form, unity, color, climax" (Butler, 1975, p. 51). *A Rhinoceros Wakes Me Up in the Morning* (Goodspeed, 1982) is a good example. The boy in the story tells about different animals who accompany him throughout his daily routines. Brilliantly colored pictures by Dennis Panek illustrate each sentence. And just when the reader and the listener are wondering if the book is pure fantasy, the story concludes with a boy tucked into bed at night, surrounded by his stuffed animal collection. The story is brought neatly to a close, yet encourages the child to review once again each animal in the book.

Note: Based on Butler (1975).

From *A Rhinoceros Wakes Me Up in the Morning* by Peter Goodspeed, illustrated by Dennis Panek. Illustration copyright © 1982 by Dennis Panek. Reproduced with permission of Bradbury Press, an Affiliate of Macmillan, Inc.

Reading the book aloud. The quickest way to learn how to read a book to a child is to watch (or hear) someone else do it. Accompany your child to a story session sponsored by the library. Watch a television series like the Public Broadcasting Service's *Reading Rainbow*. Each episode of *Reading Rainbow* includes one complete book, skillfully read, such as Jeanette Caine's (1982) *Just Us Women*. Notice how the books are shared, that they are read with expression but not overdramatized. Read the book through completely. Then sit some place quite with the child seated comfortably next to you and share the story. Pause to answer your child's questions or acknowledge his or her comments. Toddlers tend to look at a few pictures and talk about them briefly; preschoolers are generally ready for somewhat longer stories with plots. Figure 5.2 contains general guidelines for selecting books for infants, toddlers, and 3-year-olds.

Associating reading with these pleasurable feelings and the undivided attention of a caring adult is one of the ways that children learn to like reading. Children who read tend to come from a "print-rich" environment in which adults read regularly both to themselves and to their children (Stewart, 1985).

Illustration by Pat Cummings from *Just Us Women* by Jeannette Caines. Illustrations copyright © 1982 by Pat Cummings. Reprinted by permission of Harper & Row Publishers, Inc.

Make time to read regularly. Busy parents want to know how to make the most of the time spent with children. Reading to them is certainly one answer. Limit family television viewing and plan some time for reading. The International Reading Association has an important slogan: "Parents who read have children who read."

What if parents cannot read well enough to share books with children? The best answer to this question came from a participant in a workshop on children's literature. She said, "My father was illiterate, and he wanted so much for his children to be readers. Every weekend he would take us to the library. We would choose lots of different books, and he would admire our choices. I still have fond memories of those special Saturdays." In this single-parent family, being able to read was valued even though the father had never learned to read. What a strong person he must have been to admit his illiteracy, yet demand something better for his children! Until there was a reader in the house, he found relatives, friends, neighbors, and professionals who could help. But when his eldest, a 5-year-old girl, learned to read, it was a breakthrough for everyone in the family. She became the "resident reader" and shared the books they admired and wondered about. She grew up and became a Head Start aide, at-

tended college, and became a teacher. Despite the fact that their father could not read, these children came from a "print-rich" environment. They all learned not only *how* to read but to *value* reading. This father lived to see the promise of those well-spent Saturdays and his dream fulfilled: All of his children became avid readers, excelled in school, and matured into successful professionals.

If there is no time in your home for reading, then children cannot be expected to become enthusiastic readers. Choosing good books and sharing them together contributes immeasurably to the child's reading abilities.

Too much of the reading instruction in America is oriented toward remediation. We have become so preoccupied with preventing problems that new problems have been created in the process. Instead, we need to study how children learn to become literate under normal circumstances. Several such case studies have been conducted (Bissex, 1980; Butler, 1975; Calkins, 1983). The consistent message of these studies and of other research on emergent reading abilities is that literature is the perfect place to start (Teale & Sulzby, 1986). Young children seem to know that listening to stories aloud is exactly what they need in order to master the reading process. Long before they are reading independently, the words "Read me a story" and "Read it again!" are the ways in which children reach out to have their literary needs met.

Finally her mother read her a book.

"Read it again," said Emma when her mother had finished.

References

Applebee, A. N. (1978). *A child's concept of story: Ages two to five*. Chicago: University of Chicago Press.

Barton, B. (1986). *Tell me another*. Exeter, NH: Heinemann.

Bissex, G. L. (1980). *GYNS AT WRK: A child learns to write and read*. Cambridge, MA: Harvard University Press.

Butler, D. (1975). *Cushla and her books*. Boston: The Horn Book.

Calkins, L. (1983). *Lessons from a child*. Portsmouth, NH: Heinemann.

Clay, M. M. (1979). *Reading: The patterning of complex behaviour* (2nd edition). Auckland, New Zealand: Heinemann Education (NZ).

Clay, M. M. (1982). *Observing young readers*. Portsmouth, NH: Heinemann.

Cochran-Smith, M. (1984). *The making of a reader*. Norwood, NJ: Ablex.

Doake, D. (1985). Reading-like behavior: Its role in learning to read. In M. Jagger & T. Smith-Burke (Eds.), *Observing the language learner* (pp. 82–98). Newark, DE: International Reading Association.

Durkin, D. (1966). *Children who read early*. New York: Teachers College Press, Columbia University.

Erikson, E. H. (1963). *Childhood and society* (2nd ed.). New York: Norton.

Favat, F. A. (1977). *Child and tale*. Urbana, IL: National Council of Teachers of English.

Ferreiro, E., & Teberosky, A. (1982). *Literacy before schooling*. Portsmouth, NH: Heinemann.

Fields, M. (1987). *Let's begin reading right: A developmental approach to literacy*. Columbus, OH: Merrill.

Jacobs, L. (1965). *Using literature with young children*. New York: Teachers College Press, Columbia University.

"And again."

"And again."

Jewell, M.G., & Zintz, M.V. (1986). *Learning to read naturally*. Dubuque, IA: Kendall/Hunt.

Kimmel, M.M., & Segel, E. (1984). *For reading out loud! A guide to sharing books with children*. New York: Dell.

Kontos, S. (1986). What preschool children know about reading and how they learn it. *Young Children, 42*(1), 58–65.

Larrick, N. (1980). *Children's reading begins at home*. Winston-Salem, NC: Starstream Products.

Lee, O.M., & Allen, R.V. (1941). *Learning to read through experience*. New York: Appleton-Century-Crofts.

Martin, B., & Brogran, P. (1972). *Teacher's guide, instant readers*. New York: Holt, Rinehart & Winston.

McDonnell, G.M., & Osborn, E.B. (1978). New thoughts about reading readiness. *Language Arts, 55*(1), 26–29.

Silvern, S. (1985). Parent involvement and reading achievement: Research and implications for practice. *Childhood Education, 62*, 44–51.

Snow, C. (1983). Literacy and language: Relationships during the preschool years. *Harvard Educational Review, 53*, 165–189.

Stewart, I.S. (1985). Kindergarten reading curriculum: Reading abilities, not reading readiness. *Childhood Education, 61*, 356–360.

Taylor, D. (1983). *Family literacy: Young children learning to read and write*. Portsmouth, NH: Heinemann.

Teale, W.H. (1978). Positive environment for learning to read: What studies of early readers tell us. *Language Arts, 55*, 922–932.

Teale, W.H., & Sulzby, E. (Eds.). (1986). *Emergent literacy: Writing and reading*. Norwood, NJ: Ablex.

Tovey, D.R., Johnson, L.G., & Szporer, M. (1986). Remedying the 180 degree syndrome in reading. *Childhood Education, 63*, 11–15.

Trelease, J. (1985). *The read-aloud handbook*. New York: Penguin.

Willert, M.K., & Kamii, C. (1985). Reading in kindergarten: Direct vs. indirect teaching. *Young Children, 40*(4), 3–9.

Children's Books

Aardema, V. (1990). *Rabbit makes a monkey of lion*. New York: Dial.

Ackerman, K. (1989). *Song and dance man*. New York: Knopf.

Ahlberg, J., & Ahlberg, A. (1990). *Bye bye baby: A sad story with a happy ending*. Boston, MA: Little, Brown.

Baer, F. (1990). *This is the way we go to school: A book about children around the world*. New York: Scholastic.

Caines, J. (1982). *Just us women*. New York: Harper/Trophy.

Fox, M. (1989). *Night noises*. San Diego, CA: Harcourt Brace Jovanovich.

Galbraith, K.O. (1990). *Laura Charlotte*. New York: Putnam/Philomel.

Goodspeed, P. (1982). *A rhinoceros wakes me up in the morning*. New York: Bradbury.

Hale, S.J. (1990). *Mary had a little lamb*. New York: Macmillan. Photo-illustrations by B. Mc Millan.

Hooks, W.H. (1989). *The three little pigs and the fox*. New York: Macmillan.

Hutchins. P. (1971). *Rosie's walk*. New York: Macmillan.

Jonas, A. (1989). *Color dance*. New York: Greenwillow.

Luenn, N. (1990). *Nessa's fish*. New York: Atheneum.

Martin, B., & Archambault, J. (1989). *Chicka chicka boom boom*. New York: Simon & Schuster.

Mendez, P. (1990). *The black snowman*. New York: Scholastic.

Polacco, P. (1990). *Thunder cake*. New York: Putnam/Philomel.

Pomerantz, C. (1989). *The chalk doll*. New York: Lippincott.

Rosen, M. (1989). *We're going on a bear hunt*. New York: McElderry/Mcmillan.

Sendak, M. (1964). *Where the wild things are*. New York: Harper & Row.

Stock, C. (1988). *Sophie's knapsack*. New York: Lothrop, Lee & Shepard.

Viorst, J. (1971). *The tenth good thing about Barney*. New York: Atheneum.

Walsh, E.S. (1989). *Mouse paint*. San Diego, CA: Harcourt Brace Jovanovich.

Chapter 6
THE TEACHER'S ROLE IN PROMOTING PICTURE BOOKS

Books can play a significant role in the life of the young child, but the extent to which they do depends entirely upon adults . . . . The responsibility lies first with parents but is shared by child care workers, early childhood teachers, . . . and all others whose work reaches young children. There is a great store of literature to share with the young, but the wealth could go unused if adults disregard their responsibilities. Adults must sing the songs, say the rhymes, tell the tales, and read the stories to children to make literature and all its benefits central to children's lives.

Bernice E. Cullinan, Literature and Young Children*

L isten to 4-year-old Nicholas as he tells a story he has heard many times:

Once upon a time there were three bears. Mommy Bear was cooking. Baby Bear was playing. Daddy Bear was reading. The three bears sat down to eat breakfast. The cereal is too hot, so Baby Bear said, "Let's go for a walk." Then a little girl walked in. She was a bad little girl. She saw three bowls of hot cereal on the table. "I'm hungry," she said. She tasted Daddy Bear's, it's too hot. Then she tried Mommy Bear's, it's too cold. Baby Bear's was ju...uu...st right. She ate it all up shirp! She sat on Baby Bear's chair and went up and down on it, and the chair broke—pu...sh and she fell. Laid down in Daddy Bear's bed too hard. Laid down in Mommy Bear's bed too soft. "My food are all gone" and then Baby Bear starts to cry. "Somebody broke my chair! Wee! Wee! Wee! Wee! Wee! Get out of my bed," said Baby Bear. "You can't sleep all the time."

This 4-year-old's first day of nursery school was "Three Bears' Day." Nicholas felt confident and comfortable when the teacher read a lavishly illustrated version of the tale (Brett, 1987). He participated in a dramatization of the story using simple props—three different sized bowls, chairs, and rugs (to represent the beds). He followed a rebus recipe to make porridge (oatmeal with raisins) and ate some as a snack. There were teddy bears of three different sizes in the housekeeping corner. The class saw a film version of *Corduroy* (Freeman, 1976) about a small bear in search of a button for his overalls. Other books about bears such as *The Three Bears Rhyme Book* (Yolen, 1987), *Emma's Vacation* (McPhail, 1987), *Mooncake* (Asch, 1983), *Deep in the Forest* (Turkle, 1976), *Alphabears* (Hague, 1984), and *Peace at Last* (Murphy, 1980) were displayed in the reading center. One of the manipulatives used with the flannel board was a classification game where objects are arranged from smallest to largest. Two records, *Jamberry* (Degan, 1986) and *Unbearable Bears* (Roth, 1986), were in the listening center. Even the children's name tags were index cards with a small swatch of bear print fabric glued next to their names. The morning concluded with a rhythm band march to the record from the song picture book *The Teddy Bears' Picnic* (Kennedy, 1983).

"The Three Bears" from *Favorite Nursery Tales* by Tomie de Paola. Copyright © 1987 by Tomie de Paola. Reprinted by permission of the publisher, The Putnam Publishing Group.

From *The Teddy Bears' Picnic* by Jimmy Kennedy. Illustrations copyright © 1983 by Alexandra Day. Reprinted by permission of the publisher, The Green Tiger Press.

This was one teacher's interpretation of her role in promoting picture books. Complete the Self-Assessment For Teachers form (pp. 106–107) to evaluate your use of literature to enhance children's growth in literacy.

Goals for the Literature Program

The specific goals of an early childhood literature program should be consistent with the general objectives of the National Council of Teachers of English (1983), which include helping children:

- to identify with characters, understand interpersonal relationships, and gain insights from literature
- to appreciate the rhythms and beauty of language
- to understand the importance of literature as a mirror of human experience
- to develop effective ways of talking about literature
- to develop positive attitudes toward literature that carry over into adult life
- to become aware of quality books and their authors

What happens when these goals are being achieved? Listen to 7-year-old Desmond as he talks about his favorite summer reading choice, *The Turtle's Picnic* (Berger, 1977):

> They were going on a picnic and they got all the food and when they got there the little baby forgot the can opener and then he went . . . he asked his mother, father would they promise not to touch nothin' or eat something and then he act like he went home. He stayed out there for *six* years and the mother and father were waitin'. And then they got so hungry they figured, "Well, a little snack wouldn't do [any harm]." And then the father said, "No, no. We're gonna keep the promise." And then after a few hours later he said, "I guess a snack wouldn't do [any harm]." As soon as he was gettin' ready to bite, he [the little turtle] came out and said, "Ah ha!" and then he said, "You all shoulda kept your promise."

When Desmond was asked, "What do you think the writer was trying to tell you?" he answered, "If you forget something, you gotta think of it before you get there." Desmond is a good example of what a literature program should achieve. He talks easily about books, understands how literature and life are connected, and decided to join the city library's summer reading program. What can early childhood educators do to achieve these goals in their literature program?

A Role Description for Teachers

Several observational studies have identified teachers as a highly influential force in shaping children's knowledge, skills, attitudes, and habits where literature is concerned (Perez, 1986). Ideally, the teacher works to establish a classroom where books are read, discussed, recommended, and connected with other curricular areas. To accomplish this, adults must function in at least three important roles (Hickman, 1984; Stewig, 1980):

1. *As an appreciative reader of children's books.* Observational studies both at home and at school have shown that children tend to emulate adults' responses to literature (Taylor, 1983). One essential role of the teacher as a literate adult is to convince children that listening to stories, participating in discussions, learning to read, and mastering the writing process to become an author are worth all the effort. Reading aloud is one way to communicate these ideas. Children need to see adults who know and enjoy literature. In the role of appreciative reader, adults can enthusiastically recommend a book with a comment like: "Sasha, I know you like to visit your grandpa. Here's a story about a little girl who walks with her grandfather on Sunday mornings, *The Crack-of-Dawn Walkers*" (Hest, 1984).

As members of a community of readers and listeners, teachers can also point out unique aspects of books that challenge the young child, such as the detailed borders containing nursery rhyme characters in Tomie de Paola's *Favorite Nursery Tales* (1986) or the dedication page in *When I Was Young in the Mountains* (Rylant, 1982). Central to the role of an appreciative reader is the early childhood educator's enthusiasm for picture books.

2. *As a person who is responsive to children's needs and literature's potential for addressing those needs.* Adults exert a major influence on the child's perceptions of literature when they select books, structure the story session, determine the focus, and identify appropriate questions. When adults do not allow time to discuss a book, or, conversely, discuss the story in a very regimented way, children may miss the richness of literature. As Petrosky (1980) observes:

> Books are worlds. Books are experiences. Children need to talk with each other and with teachers about their encounters with those worlds, those experiences. We would do well to minimize our expectations of quick answers and fast responses. Meaning comes slowly. . . . We need to encourage children to talk to us and to each other about what they see, feel, think, and how they associate with what they read. (p. 155)

3. *As an advocate for literature in the early childhood curriculum.* Adults are also responsible for structuring the physical environment for literacy development. Making books and related materials available to children is an important first step. Some classrooms and centers are stocked with a few battered copies of the books found in discount stores. Although some books are probably better than none, these stories are not representative of the best that picture books have to offer. How can teachers with limited budgets get quality literature into children's hands? Four ways to achieve this goal are:

USE THE PUBLIC LIBRARY. Librarians want picture books to be circulated to the public. Some communities even have a librarian who specializes in literature for children. Even if the local library is small, it may have cooperative arrangements with larger branches and be able to obtain what you need. Establishing a good working relationship with a professional who keeps up to date with picture books can improve the literature curriculum.

SUBSTITUTE BOOKS FOR SNACKS. It is customary in many schools for a child to bring a treat on his or her birthday. Instead of a sugary snack, one school set a policy that children would donate a picture book to the classroom library. The inside cover of each book had a card that read:

Donated by ————————————— to —————————————
School on ——————, 19———.

Because the teacher had shared lists of recommended picture books and best picture books in paperback with parents, most of the donations to the classroom library were not only appropriate but also approximately the same price as candy or cupcakes for the class. Within 5 years, the classroom library had acquired almost one hundred favorite picture books.

USE COMMUNITY RESOURCES. Early childhood educators need to publicize the fact that they are in the process of building a classroom library. The school or center's newsletter, an ad in the local newspaper, or a public service message on the radio or television can publicize the project. One Head Start teacher made this a project for several parent volunteers. They were responsible for advertising for, obtaining, and screening the books that were contributed. A director of a private child care center recruited two parents who enjoyed frequenting garage sales. They were coached on the types of books to select and used the proceeds from a bake sale to purchase their finds. A teacher in a cooperative nursery school found a grandparent who would build a bookcase and visit the children several times to demonstrate the basics of woodworking.

CREATE BOOKS WITH THE CHILDREN. Another way to expand the book collection is by having children dictate their own stories. Their books can be printed or typed by an adult, illustrated and signed by the child. Beginning writers can create books in which each child contributes one page if an entire story seems overwhelming. If children are not yet drawing representationally, photographs or pictures cut out from magazines can be used as illustrations. Children are interested in what other children have to say and the pictures they draw, so they are motivated to read these homemade books.

Designing original picture books also gives children a renewed appreciation for the task facing authors and illustrators. Older children may even take on a challenge like inventing their own versions of books with unique formats. Some second graders created a lift-the-flap book similar to Eric Hill's (1980) *Where's Spot?* and presented one of their creations each day to a group of kindergartners in their elementary school.

Teacher Advocacy for Literature

When teachers set aside time for literature, present books in an engaging way, set children's expectations for books, and extend literature into other curricular areas, they let children know that books are important. There is physical evidence of taking time for books — such as a library and classroom display of children's responses to literature. There is evidence of special places for sharing literature too — such as a semicircular seating arrangement marked on the floor with carpet squares, or a comfortable rocking chair. Extensions of literature are apparent as well — props to encourage dramatization of the story, such as a stack of hats to be used in enacting *Caps for Sale* (Slobodkin, 1940) or masks to wear when dramatizing *Who's In Rabbit's House?* (Aardema, 1977). All of these teacher-advocacy behaviors set the stage for a literature-based curriculum.

A Literature-Based Curriculum

The National Commission on Reading issued their report on the status of literacy in America, *Becoming a Nation of Readers*. Following an exhaustive review of the literature, they concluded:

The single most important activity for building the knowledge required for eventual success in reading is reading aloud to children. . . . The benefits are greatest when the child is an active participant, discussing stories, identifying letters and words, and talking about the meaning of words. (Anderson, Hiebert, Scott, & Wilkinson, 1985, p. 23)

Margaret Meek (1982) summarized her research on reading by saying that "children learn to read by interaction with what *they believe to be significant texts*" (p. 14). In other words, most children learn to read from pleasurable experiences with favorite picture books. How does literature become such an essential part of children's lives? The relationship between music and literature provides a useful analogy. Both are art forms, both have a language, and both have appreciation as their ultimate goal. Young children learn to love music by participation—listening and singing along before they attempt to read or play music. Teaching every young child the intricacies of musical notation would be considered inappropriate because it is assumed that enjoyment is the place to begin.

Unfortunately, where learning to read is concerned, just the opposite assumption is often made. Americans tend to begin with bits of language (the letters of the alphabet, sight words, vowel sounds) and try to convince the children to stay interested until they know enough to put the pieces together. Figure 6.1 compares/contrasts the literature-based and textbook-based approaches.

Figure 6.1
A Comparison of Literature- and Textbook-Based Programs

	Literature-based	Textbook-based
Assumption	learning to read is natural, enjoyable	learning to read is difficult, technical
View of the child	the child is actively constructing meaning from literature; emphasis is on building upon what the child knows	the child is passively receiving formal reading instruction; emphasis is on what the child does not know
Approach	entire stories ("whole language") are the place to begin	the smallest components—letters, words and short sentences—are the appropriate starting place
Selection of material	adults and children select material	textbook publisher selects material
Curricular implications	picture books are the central focus; they are the basis for reading, writing, speaking and listening activities	picture books are peripheral; dittos and workbooks occupy most of children's time

Theory Into Practice

How does a literature-based early childhood program work? Its basic premise is that learning to read should follow the same progression that has been observed in young children who read early (Allen, 1984; Fields & Lee, 1987). A literature-based program begins by sharing many stories with children. Often these stories are in big book format — a poster-sized book that enables a group of children to see the pictures and the print (see Bridge, 1986; Heald-Taylor, 1987; Tovey, Johnson, & Szporer, 1988). Based upon Sulzby's (1985) research, the sequence of the emergent reading program begins with children discussing the pictures and gradually moves toward independent reading. She refers to it as moving from "picture-governed attempts" at reading to "text-governed attempts." Here is Julio, a 34-month-old, relying much more on pictures than on text:

Spot Goes to the Circus*
(Hill, 1980)

Page	Text of the book	Julio, 34 months old
		(Reads title) Spot Goes to the Circus
	(Mother) Fetch your ball, Spot. We're at the circus.	That's Spot and his mommy.
1	(Clown) It's okay, I've got it. That's my nose, silly.	Town talked to Spot.
3	Excuse me, did you see my ball go by?	
4	(Elephant) I don't think so.	Spot talkin' to efant.
5	There it goes! I wonder who lives in here.	
6	You're a brave pup.	It's a gurilla. A lion. It's a tider.
7	Please, do you have my ball?	It's a bear standin' on de horse.
8	(Kangaroo) You just missed it.	
9	I hope you didn't swallow my ball.	
10	(Looking in the lion's mouth) I can't see it.	Spot in der, in lion's mouse. I like that lion, he's scared . . .
18	(Seal) It's easy, try it.	Seal has ball on nose. That's the end.
19	(Mother) Spot, who taught you how to do that? (Spot) My friend the seal. It's easy.	(Julio points to Spot) That's on his nose.
		(Julio concludes by pointing to Sally, the mother in the story, and then to his own mother.)

* From Spot Goes to the Circus by Eric Hill. Copyright © 1980 by Eric Hill. Reprinted by permission of the publisher, The Putnam Publishing Group.

Kayla, a 4-year-old, uses a more text-governed approach to tell *The Doorbell Rang* (Hutchins, 1986). Notice how closely her words follow the language of the story:

The Doorbell Rang*
(Hutchins, 1986)

Page	Text of the book	Kayla, 4 years old
1	"I've made some cookies for tea," said Ma. "Good," said Victoria and Sam. "We're starving." "Share them between yourselves," said Ma. "I made plenty."	"I made cookies," said Mom. "Good," said Sam. Mom said, "Share dem."
2	"That's six each," said Sam and Victoria. "They look as good as Grandma's," said Victoria. "They smell as good as Grandma's," said Sam.	"We can have some. They wook like Grama's. They smell like Grama's."
3	"No one makes cookies like Grandma," said Ma as the doorbell rang.	"No one makes cookies like Grama."
4	It was Tom and Hannah from next door. "Come in," said Ma. "You can share the cookies."	Tom an Anna came over to have cookies.
6	"That's three each," said Sam and Victoria. "They smell as good as your Grandma's," said Tom. "And look as good," said Hannah.	"That's six each. They smell like Grama's."
7	"No one makes cookies like Grandma," said Ma as the door bell rang.	"No one makes cookies like Grama."
18	"Oh dear," said Ma as the children stared at the cookies on their plates.	The kids looked at their plates.
19	"Perhaps you'd better eat them before we open the door." "We'll wait," said Sam.	"Don't open the door," said Sam.
20	It was Grandma with an enormous tray of cookies.	It was Grama!
21	"How nice to have so many friends to share them with," said Grandma. "It's a good thing I made a lot!"	She has lots of cookies.
22	"And no one makes cookies like Grandma," said Ma as the doorbell rang.	"No one makes cookies like Grama."

* From *The Doorbell Rang* by Pat Hutchins. Copyright © 1986 by Pat Hutchins. Reprinted by permission of the publisher, Greenwillow Books (A division of William Morrow & Company, Inc.).

An ability like Kayla's was once disregarded as simple memorization. Researchers now corroborate what expert teachers have known intuitively all along: This reading-like behavior is as closely related to learning to read as walking with support is to walking unassisted (Doake, 1985; Teale & Sulzby, 1986).

The young child who is not yet reading independently is receiving more attention in the research. It used to be that reading, defined as accurately decoding words, was the only phenomenon considered worthy of serious study. Similarly, because literary appreciation could not be observed or measured easily, it was neglected. Recent research has enabled us to better understand the process of learning to read and to understand how literary appreciation is a direct outgrowth of early experiences with books.

Even the terminology is different. Rather than *reading readiness,* which connotes children in a holding pattern before "real" reading, the terminology has been changed to *reading abilities* (Stewart, 1985), *emergent reading* (Sulzby, 1985), or *emergent literacy* (Holdaway, 1979).

The premise of using an oversized book with groups of preschoolers and children in the primary grades is that the process used with the group most closely approximates the process children learn at home.

A shared book experience follows this basic sequence:

Introduction
Select a book with repetition, rhyme, simple plot, and/or predictable text. Familiarize children with the book using a big book, transparencies, or charts. Discuss pictures, ask and answer questions.

Practice
Read the book twice, asking children to join in wherever possible. Read the book in unison, encouraging children to participate at their own level.
Teach skills as children inquire about them.

Extension
Incorporate other activities such as dramatization; listening to audiotapes; children reading in pairs or small groups; children dictating, illustrating, and reading their own stories.

Independence
Encourage children to read the book to a partner or partners.
Give children small paperback copies to read.
Allow children to select other predictable books to read.

Consider for a moment some of the advantages of the shared book experience:

- It permits children to participate at their own level and to experience success

- It is an enjoyable activity that provides practice in prereading and reading abilities
- It uses whole language and quality literature as the reading material rather than a stilted vocabulary based on a few sight words.

(For more detailed information on the use of oversized picture books, consult Barrett, 1972 or Heald-Taylor, 1987.)

Picture Books To Build Curriculum

Teachers can brainstorm for ideas, design related activities, and plan entire units by beginning with a picture book. Three basic approaches to literature curriculum building will be discussed here: developmental themes, graphic organizers, and subject areas.

By focusing on developmental issues that most members of an age group face, teachers can plan a well-coordinated sequence of story choices. Figure 6.2 illustrates one such plan based upon the themes from *Sheila Rae, the Brave* (Henkes, 1987).

A second technique for building a literature-based curriculum is to use a graphic organizer. There are many different ways to chart ideas and their relationships (Bromley, 1988; Cullinan, 1987). The web, one kind of graphic organizer, begins with a topic and charts other ideas related to the topic, categorizing each in a logical way. A web on the topic of sleep is contained in Figure 6.3.

A third strategy for designing a literature-based curriculum is to designate the *traditional subject areas* and list related activities under each subject heading (Figure 6.4).

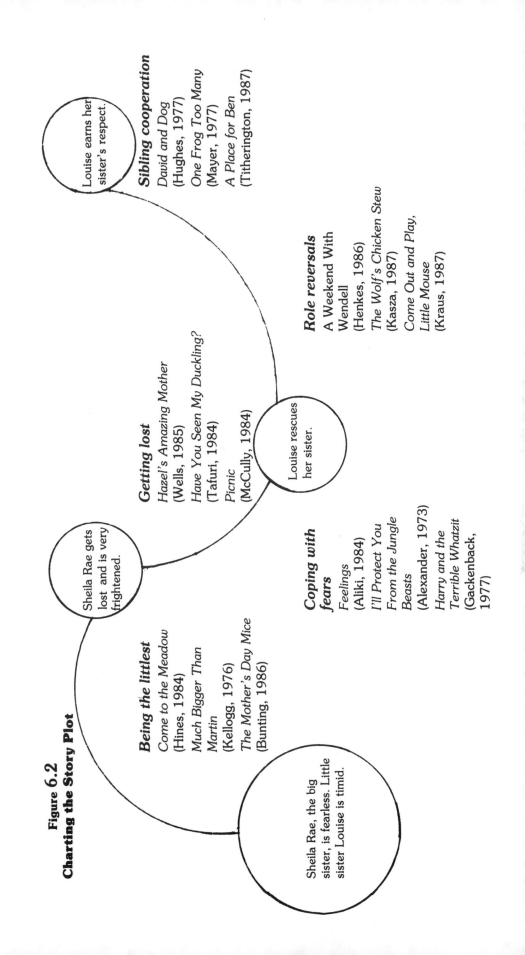

Figure 6.2
Charting the Story Plot

Sheila Rae, the big sister, is fearless. Little sister Louise is timid.

Being the littlest
Come to the Meadow
(Hines, 1984)
Much Bigger Than
Martin
(Kellogg, 1976)
The Mother's Day Mice
(Bunting, 1986)

Sheila Rae gets lost and is very frightened.

Getting lost
Hazel's Amazing Mother
(Wells, 1985)
Have You Seen My Duckling?
(Tafuri, 1984)
Picnic
(McCully, 1984)

Coping with fears
Feelings
(Aliki, 1984)
I'll Protect You
From the Jungle
Beasts
(Alexander, 1973)
Harry and the
Terrible Whatzit
(Gackenback,
1977)

Louise rescues her sister.

Role reversals
A Weekend With
Wendell
(Henkes, 1986)
The Wolf's Chicken Stew
(Kasza, 1987)
Come Out and Play,
Little Mouse
(Kraus, 1987)

Louise earns her sister's respect.

Sibling cooperation
David and Dog
(Hughes, 1977)
One Frog Too Many
(Mayer, 1977)
A Place for Ben
(Titherington, 1987)

Figure 6.3
A Web Using Picture Books Suggestions for 1-, 2-, and 3-year olds

| Getting ready for bed |

| Bathing and changing clothes |

Bathwater's Hot
(Hughes, 1985)
I Dance in My Red Pajamas
(Hurd, 1982)
All By Myself
(Hines, 1985)

| Toys and blankets |

Max's Bedtime
(Wells, 1985)
When I'm Sleepy
(Howard, 1986)
The Quilt Story
(Johnston, 1985)

| Poetry |

When the Dark Comes Dancing
(Larrick, 1983)
Night in the Country
(Rylant, 1986)
*Jump All the Morning: A Child's
Day in Verse*
(Roche, 1984)
Wynken, Blynken and Nod
(Field, 1982)

| Sleep |

When Sheep Cannot Sleep
(Kitamura, 1987)
Moonlight
(Omerod, 1982)
Roll over!
(Gerstein, 1984)

| Pleasant Dreams |

Wolf's Dream
(Tejima, 1988)
The Donkey's Dream
(Berger, 1985)
Close Your Eyes
(Marzollo, 1978)
If There Were Dreams To Sell
(Lalicki, 1984)

| Waking up |

Jesse Bear, What Will You Wear?
(Carlstrom, 1986)
Early Morning in the Barn
(Tafuri, 1982)
How Do I Put It On?
(Wantanabe, 1979)

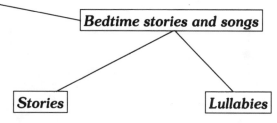

Bedtime stories and songs

Stories

The Baby's Lap Book
(Chorao, 1977)
Calf, Goodnight
(Jewell, 1973)
Midnight Farm
(Lindbergh, 1987)

Lullabies

All the Pretty Horses
(Jeffers, 1974)
Lullabies and Laughter
(Carfra, 1987)
Once: A Lullaby
(Nichol, 1986)
The Lullaby Songbook
(Yolen, 1986)

Nightmares

There's an Alligator Under My Bed
(Mayer, 1987)
No Elephants Allowed
(Robinson, 1981)
What's Under My Bed?
(Stevenson, 1983)

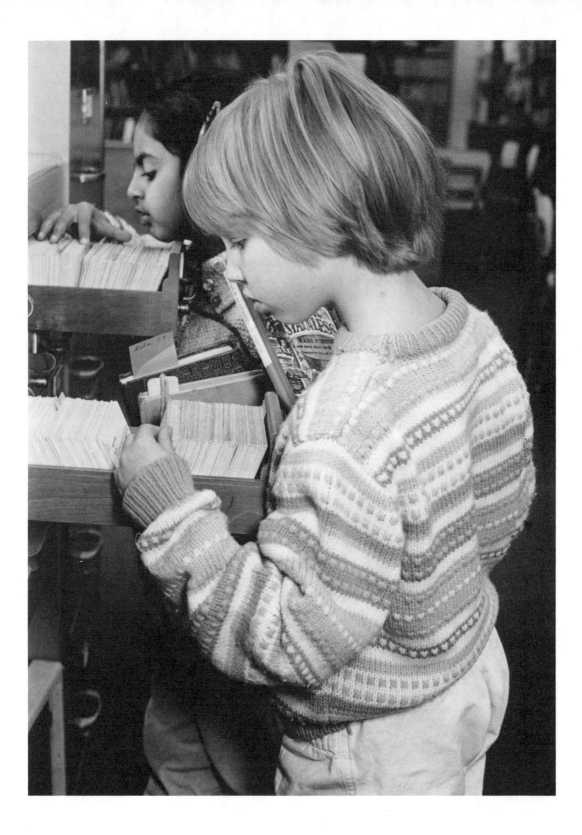

The Biggest Pumpkin Ever
(Kroll, 1984)
Suggested activities for 4-, 5-, and 6-year-olds

Language arts
- listen to a tape recording of Hal Linden reading the story (Kroll, 1986)
- read the poem "Mice" by Rose Fyleman (1969)
- share other stories about mice: *The Mother's Day Mice* (Bunting, 1986), *Come Out and Play, Little Mouse* (Kraus, 1987), *Sheila Rae, the Brave* (Henkes, 1987), *Mousekin's Golden House* (Miller, 1964), *Frederick* (Lionni, 1985)
- read other books about gigantic food like *Cloudy With a Chance of Meatballs* (Barrett, 1978)

Science
- visit a pumpkin patch
- experiment with sugar water as a way of stimulating a pumpkin's growth
- carve a jack-o'-lantern
- observe a real mouse and its proportion in relationship to a large pumpkin
- look for the first frost in the fall
- read a story about the seasons of the year such as *A Year of Beasts* (Wolff, 1986)

Nutrition/cooking
- roast and salt pumpkin seeds
- make pumpkin pie or pumpkin bread by following a rebus recipe
- cook pumpkin soup using a recipe from the Colonial American era

Mathematics
- use magnetic geometric shapes and a pizza pan painted with lead-free orange paint to create different jack-o'-lantern faces
- have the children create a bulletin board to show the 100 mice on motorcycles; read *Anno's Counting Book* (Anno, 1977), *How Much Is a Million?* (Schwartz, 1985)
- use children's drawings of pumpkins to categorize as small, medium, or large
- play a seriation game in which pumpkins drawn by the children are arranged from the smallest and greenest to largest and most orange

Aesthetics
- create mouse finger puppets using peanut shells, finger tips from old gloves, or felt
- use modeling dough to create something from the story
- sing and dramatize "In My Garden" and "Down on Grandpa's Farm" by Raffi (1985)
- sing the song picture book, *The Fox Went Out on a Chilly Night* (Spier, 1961)

Social studies
- coach children in role playing the scene where the two mice decide to share the pumpkin
- discuss *Best Friends* (Kellogg, 1986) and the girls' decision to share the puppy

When the celebration was over, the hundred field mice pulled the pumpkin back to the field. The day before Halloween, they carved it into the best jack-o'-lantern ever.

CHILDREN'S LITERATURE IN THE CLASSROOM: A SELF-ASSESSMENT FOR TEACHERS

Instructions: Respond to each of these items by indicating how often it occurs in your classroom: almost always, frequently, occasionally, seldom, or almost never.

	5 Almost always	4 Frequently	3 Occasionally	2 Seldom	1 Almost never
1. I set aside time for reading aloud to children each day.	( )	( )	( )	( )	( )
2. I prepare for the use of picture books by reading them in advance.	( )	( )	( )	( )	( )
3. I introduce stories with a motivational technique.	( )	( )	( )	( )	( )
4. I relate children's books to other curricular areas.	( )	( )	( )	( )	( )
5. I supplement the center's or school's collection with books borrowed from the library and other sources.	( )	( )	( )	( )	( )
6. I use community resources such as librarians, parents, and other volunteers to enhance the children's literature program.	( )	( )	( )	( )	( )
7. I encourage children to discuss picture books during storytime.	( )	( )	( )	( )	( )
8. I keep current in children's literature through participation in professional conferences, reading book reviews, in-service training, and/or college coursework.	( )	( )	( )	( )	( )
9. When requested, I offer assistance to parents in choosing appropriate books for their children.	( )	( )	( )	( )	( )
10. I make a special effort to locate books that are relevant to classroom activities or to the interests of individual children.	( )	( )	( )	( )	( )

	5 Almost always	4 Frequently	3 Occasionally	2 Seldom	1 Almost never
11. I prepare supplemental materials to accompany children's books such as puppets, dioramas, book displays, and activity boards.	( )	( )	( )	( )	( )
12. I tell (rather than read) familiar stories to children.	( )	( )	( )	( )	( )
13. I encourage children's artistic responses to literature (art, drama, dance).	( )	( )	( )	( )	( )
14. I praise children's efforts to properly care for books.	( )	( )	( )	( )	( )
15. I have an area in my classroom that is designated for reading and listening to books and records.	( )	( )	( )	( )	( )
16. I select books that represent diversity in style, format, illustration, and literary genre.	( )	( )	( )	( )	( )
17. The picture books I read depict ethnic groups, minorities, religious groups, females, and the handicapped in positive, active roles.	( )	( )	( )	( )	( )
18. I enjoy sharing picture books with young children.	( )	( )	( )	( )	( )
19. I respect children's preferences and permit them to choose books to be read.	( )	( )	( )	( )	( )
20. I can identify from memory several outstanding children's book authors and illustrators.	( )	( )	( )	( )	( )

Scoring: Each item is phrased positively so a perfect score is 5×20 or 100.

85–100 Excellent
75–80 Good
65–70 Average

References

Allen, J. (1984). The bottom-up deficit myth: Analysis of a language experience reader. *Journal of Language Experience, 6,* 19–25.

Anderson, R.C., Hiebert, E. H., Scott, J. A., & Wilkinson, I. A. G. (1985). *Becoming a nation of readers: The report of the Commission on Reading.* Washington, DC: U.S. Office of Education.

Barrett, T. C. (1972). *A taxonomy of reading comprehension.* (Reading 360 Monograph) Lexington, MA: Ginn.

Bridge, C. (1986). *Predictable books for beginning readers and writers.* In M. Sampson (Ed.), *The pursuit of literacy: Early reading and writing* (pp. 81–96). Dubuque, IA: Kendall/Hunt.

Bromley, K. D. (1988). *Language arts: Early reading and writing.* Dubuque, IA: Kendall/Hunt.

Cullinan, B. (1987). *Literature and the child.* New York: Harcourt Brace Jovanovich.

Doake, D. (1985). Reading-like behavior: Its role in learning to read. In M. Jagger & T. Smith-Burke (Eds.), *Observing the language learner* (pp. 82–98). Newark, DE: International Reading Association.

Fields, M., & Lee, D. (1987). *Let's begin reading right: A developmental approach to beginning literacy.* Columbus, OH: Merrill.

Heald-Taylor, G. (1987). How to use predictable books for K–2 language arts instruction. *The Reading Teacher, 40,* 656–661.

Hickman, J. (1984). Research currents: Researching children's response to literature. *Language Arts, 61,* 278–284.

Holdaway, D. (1979). *The foundations of literacy.* New York: Ashton/Scholastic.

Meek, M. (Ed.). (1982). *The cool web: The patterning of children's reading.* London: Bodley Head.

National Council of Teachers of English. (1983). A statement on the preparation of teachers of English and the language arts. Forum: Essentials of English. *Language Arts, 60,* 244–248.

Perez, S. A. (1986). Children see, children do: Teachers as reading models. *The Reading Teacher, 40,* 8–11.

Petrosky, A. R. (1980). The inferences we make: Children and literature. *Language Arts, 57,* 149–156.

Stewart, I.S. (1985). Kindergarten reading curriculum abilities, not reading readiness. *Childhood Education, 61,* 356–360.

Stewig, J. W. (1980). *Children and literature.* Boston: Houghton Mifflin.

Sulzby, E. (1985). Children's emergent reading of favorite storybooks: A developmental study. *Reading Research Quarterly, 20,* 458–481.

Taylor, D. (1983). *Family literacy.* Portsmouth, NH: Heinemann.

Teale, W., & Sulzby, E. (Eds.). (1986). *Emergent literacy: Writing and reading.* Norwood, NJ: Ablex.

Tovey, D. R., Johnson, L. A., & Szporer, M. (1988). Beginning reading: A natural language learning process. *Childhood Education, 64,* 288–293.

Children's Books

Aardema, V. (1977). *Who's in rabbit's house?* New York: Dial.

Alexander, M. (1973). *I'll protect you from the jungle beasts.* New York: Dial.

Aliki. (1984). *Feelings.* New York: Greenwillow.

Anno, M. (1977). *Anno's counting book.* New York: Crowell.

Asch, F. (1983). *Mooncake*. Englewood Cliffs, NJ: Prentice-Hall.

Barrett, J. (1978). *Cloudy with a chance of meatballs*. New York: Atheneum.

Berger, B. (1985). *The donkey's dream*. New York: Philomel.

Berger, T. (1977). *The turtle's picnic*. New York: Crown.

Brett, J. (1987). *Goldilocks and the three bears*. New York: Dodd.

Bunting, E. (1986). *The mother's day mice*. New York: Clarion.

Carlstrom, N. (1986). *Jesse Bear, what will you wear?* New York: Macmillan.

Chorao, K. (1977). *The baby's lap book*. New York: Dutton.

de Paola, T. (1986). *Favorite Nursery Tales*. New York: Putnam.

Field, E. (1982). *Wynken, blynken and nod*. New York: Dutton.

Freeman, D. (1976). *Corduroy*. New York: Puffin.

Fyleman, R. (1969). Mice. In B. DeRegniers, E. Moore, & M. White (Eds.),
    Poems children will sit still for (p. 63). New York: Citation.

Gackenback, D. (1977). *Harry and the terrible whatzit*. Somers, CT: Seabury.

Gerstein, M. (1984). *Roll over!* New York: Crown.

Hague, K. (1984). *Alphabears*. New York: Holt, Rinehart & Winston.

Henkes, K. (1986). *A weekend with Wendell*. New York: Greenwillow.

Henkes, K. (1987). *Sheila Rae, the brave*. New York: Greenwillow.

Hest, A. (1984). *The crack-of-dawn walkers*. New York: Macmillan.

Hill, E. (1980). *Spot goes to the circus*. New York: Putnam.

Hill, E. (1980). *Where's Spot?* New York: Putnam.

Hines, A. G. (1984). *Come to the meadow*. New York: Clarion.

Hines, A. G. (1985). *All by myself*. New York: Clarion.

Howard, J. R. (1986). *When I'm sleepy*. New York: Dutton.

Hughes, S. (1977). *David and dog*. Englewood Cliffs, NJ: Prentice-Hall.

Hughes, S. (1985). *Bathwater's hot*. New York: Lothrop, Lee & Shepard.

Hurd, E. T. (1982). *I dance in my red pajamas*. New York: Harper & Row.

Hutchins, P. (1986). *The doorbell rang*. New York: Greenwillow.

Jeffers, S. (1974). *All the pretty horses*. New York: Macmillan.

Jewell, N. (1973). *Calf, goodnight*. New York: Harper & Row.

Johnston, T. (1985). *The quilt story*. New York: Putnam.

Kasza, K. (1987). *The wolf's chicken stew*. New York: Putnam.

Kellogg, S. (1976). *Much bigger than Martin*. New York: Dial.

Kellogg, S. (1986). *Best friends*. New York: Dial.

Kennedy, J. (1983). *The teddy bears' picnic*. La Jolla, CA: Green Tiger Press.

Kitamura, S. (1987). *When sheep cannot sleep*. New York: Farrar,
    Straus & Giroux.

Kraus, R. (1987). *Come out and play, little mouse*. New York: Greenwillow.

Kroll, S. (1984). *The biggest pumpkin ever*. New York: Holiday House.

Lalicki, B. (1984). *If there were dreams to sell*. New York: Lothrop,
    Lee & Shepard.

Larrick, N. (Ed.). (1983). *When the dark comes dancing: A bedtime poetry
    book*. New York: Putnam.

Lindbergh, R. (1987). *Midnight farm*. New York: Dutton.

Lionni, L. (1985). Frederick. In *Frederick's fables: A Leo Lionni treasury of
    favorite stories*. New York: Random House.

Marzollo, J. (1978). *Close your eyes*. New York: Dial.

Mayer, M. (1977). *One frog too many*. New York: Dial.

Mayer, M. (1987). *There's an alligator under my bed*. New York: Dial.

McCully, E. A. (1984). *Picnic*. New York: Harper & Row.

McPhail, D. (1987). *Emma's vacation*. New York: Dutton.

Miller, E. (1964). *Mousekin's golden house.* Englewood Cliffs, NJ: Prentice-Hall.

Murphy, J. (1980). *Peace at last.* New York: Dial.

Nichol, B.P. (1986). *Once: A lullaby.* New York: Greenwillow.

Omerod, J. (1982). *Moonlight.* New York: Viking/Penguin.

Robinson, D. (1981). *No elephants allowed.* Boston: Houghton Mifflin.

Roche, P.K. (1984). *Jump all the morning: A child's day in verse.* New York: Viking.

Rylant, C. (1982). *When I was young in the mountains.* New York: Dutton.

Rylant, C. (1986). *Night in the country.* New York: Bradbury.

Schwartz, D.M. (1985). *How much is a million?* New York: Lothrop, Lee & Shepard.

Slobodkin, E. (1940). *Caps for sale.* New York: Scholastic.

Spier, P. (1961). *The fox went out on a chilly night.* New York: Doubleday.

Stevenson, J. (1983). *What's under my bed?* New York: Greenwillow.

Tafuri, N. (1984). *Have you seen my duckling?* New York: Greenwillow.

Tejima. (1988). *Wolf's dream.* New York: Philomel.

Titherington, J. (1987). *A place for Ben.* New York: Greenwillow.

Turkle, B. (1976). *Deep in the forest.* New York: Dutton.

Wantanabe, S. (1979). *How do I put it on?* New York: Philomel.

Wells, R. (1985). *Max's bedtime.* New York: Dial.

Wells, R. (1985). *Hazel's amazing mother.* New York: Dial.

Wolff, A. (1986). *A year of beasts.* New York: Dutton.

Yolen, J. (Ed.). (1986). *The lullaby songbook.* New York: Harcourt Brace Jovanovich.

Yolen, J. (1987). *The three bears rhyme book.* New York: Harcourt Brace Jovanovich.

Children's Records

Carfra, P. (1987). *Lullabies and laughter.* Scarborough, Ontario: A & M Records of Canada.

Degan, B. (1986). *Jamberry.* Ancramdale, NY: Live Oak Media.

Kroll, S. (1986). *The biggest pumpkin ever.* New York: Caedmon.

Raffi. (1985). "In My Garden" and "Down on Grandpa's Farm" on *One light, one sun.* Hollywood, CA: A & M Records.

Roth, K. (1986). *Unbearable bears.* Kennett Square, PA: Marlboro Records.

Reference Books and Annotated Bibliographies

Freeman, J. (1990). *Books kids will sit still for: The complete read-aloud guide.* New York: Bowker.

Gillespie, J.T., & Naden, C.J. (1990). *Best books for children: Preschool through middle grades* (4th ed.). New York: Bowker.

Kimmel, M.M., & Segal, E. (1990). *For reading out loud!* New York: Delacorte.

Lima, C.W., & Lima, J.A. (1989). *A to Zoo: Subject access to children's picture books* (3rd ed.). New York: Bowker.

Sierra, J., & Kaminski, R. (1991). *Twice upon a time: Stories to tell, retell, act out, and write about.* Bronx, NY: Wilson.

Trelease, J. (1989). *The new read-aloud handbook.* New York: Penguin.

CONCLUSION

Literature makes an immense contribution not only to *learning* to read, but also to *liking* to read. Early childhood educators are in the position of shaping young children's attitudes toward literature. This position is in some ways enviable and in some ways frustrating. It is enviable in the sense that our influence reverberates throughout the child's lifetime; it is frustrating in the sense that so many others try to influence our decisions.

There are the sooner-the-better types who take pride in a toddler conditioned to memorize a few words on flashcards. There are the profiteers who have everything to gain from making the early childhood curriculum whatever package their company sells. There are the technologists who think that sophisticated machines are superior to a caring adult and a bedtime story.

And then there is the issue of preparing the child for the next educational experience. Should an early childhood literacy curriculum mimic the one that children are apt to encounter in grade school? Will it make the transition easier for young children if workbooks, dittos, phonics, and "reading readiness" are standard fare? Early childhood educators often pose questions like these. The query can be stated in another way: Which is more important, remaining consistent or meeting developmental needs? Andrew Stibbs (1979) places the entire issue in perspective when he says that climbing a tree is a better analogy for the development of language than climbing a ladder. When adults are too directive, they sometimes push at the wrong time, or overlook strides that need immediate support.

Even though others mistakenly treat literacy as if it were a tidy, sequential process, early childhood educators should not operate under the same misconception, as it is not in the best interest of young children. Educators of young children must base their professional decisions on 1) developmental theory; 2) a rich heritage of observation, creativity, and trial and error through which several generations of expert nursery, kindergarten, and first grade teachers have learned how literacy emerges; and 3) the most recent research on emergent literacy (Salinger, 1988). We need to emphasize what children know in a literacy curriculum rather than rely on excessively narrow and highly questionable models of what literacy is and how it functions (Hall, 1987). Our knowledge of child development, our collective professional judgment about what is right for children — these should be the driving force behind the decision to make books an integral part of daily classroom existence.

Young children need literature and, as listeners or emergent readers, they depend upon adults to explore and enjoy picture books with them. After young children have amassed many such experiences, they begin to take the lead. Usually these preschoolers become the same school-age children and adolescents who not only learn to read but also want to read. They mature into adults who value literature, parents and teachers who have the wherewithall to suggest "let's read a story" instead of switching on the television set or distributing another coloring book page. Then, because experiences with literature have reverberated throughout their lives, these adults feel pleasantly obliged to introduce the next generation of children to the world of literature. Thus, the cycle ends where it began—with enjoyment, with picture books.

References

Hall, N. (1987). *The emergence of literacy.* Portsmouth, NH: Heinemann.
Salinger, T. (1988). *Language arts and literacy for young children.* Columbus, OH: Merrill.
Stibbs, A. (1979). *Assessing children's language: Guidelines for teachers.* London: Ward Lock Educational.

More Children's Books

Bang, M. (1991). *Yellow ball.* New York: Morrow.
Barracca, D., & Barracca, S. (1990). *The adventures of Taxi dog.* New York: Dial.
Barton, B. (1990). *Bones, bones, dinosaur bones.* New York: Harper/Collins.
Brett, J. (1989). *The mitten.* New York: Putnam.
Carle, E. (1990). *The very quiet cricket.* New York: Putnam/Philomel.
Christelow, E. (1991). *Five little monkeys sitting in a tree.* New York: Clarion.
Ehlert, L. (1990). *Feathers for lunch.* San Diego, CA: Harcourt Brace Jovanovich.
Ehlert, L. (1991). *Red leaf, yellow leaf.* San Diego, CA: Harcourt Brace Jovanovich.
Hutchins, P. (1989). *Which witch is which?* New York: Greenwillow.
Henkes, K. (1990). *Julius the baby of the world.* New York: Greenwillow.
Howard, E.F. (1989). *Chita's Christmas tree.* New York: Bradbury.
Lindbergh, R. (1990). *Benjamin's barn.* New York: Dial.
Noll, S. (1990). *Watch where you go.* New York: Greenwillow.
Prelutsky, J. (1990). *Something big has been here.* New York: Greenwillow.
Wells, R. (1991). *Max's dragon shirt.* New York: Dial.
William, S. (1990). *I went walking.* San Diego, CA: Harcourt Brace Jovanovich.
Williams, V.B. (1990). *"More, more, more!" said the baby.* New York: Greenwillow.
Williamsom, K.L. (1990). *Galimoto.* New York: Lothrop, Lee & Shepard.
Wood, D., & Wood, A. (1991). *Piggies.* San Diego, CA: Harcourt Brace Jovanovich.
Zelinsky, P.O. (1990). *The wheels on the bus.* New York: Dutton.

Appendix A
OUTSTANDING PICTURE BOOK AUTHORS AND ILLUSTRATORS

Ahlberg, Allan, and
Ahlberg, Janet
Alexander, Martha
Aliki
Allard, Harry
Anno, Mitsumaso
Asch, Frank
Brett, Jan
Bridwell, Norman
Brown, Margaret Wise
Bruna, Dick
Caines, Jeannette
Carle, Eric
Cauley, Lorinda Bryan
Chorao, Kay
Cleary, Beverly
Cohen, Miriam
Cole, Joanna
Conover, Chris
Crews, Donald
Degen, Bruce
de Paola, Tomie
Emberly, Ed
Flack, Marjorie
Giff, Patricia Reilly
Gackenbach, Dick
Goode, Diane
Greenfield, Eloise
Hall, Donald
Hazen, Barbara
Henkes, Kevin
Hest, Amy
Hoban, Lillian and
Hoban, Russell
Hoban, Tana
Hoberman, Mary Ann
Hafner, Marilyn
Hughes, Shirley
Hutchins, Pat
Jeffers, Susan
Keats, Ezra Jack
Kellogg, Steven

Lionni, Leo
Lobel, Arnold
Locker, Thomas
Marshall, James
Mayer, Marianna and
Mayer, Mercer
McCloskey, Robert
McPhail, David
Merriam, Eve
Milne, A. A.
Omerod, Jan
Oxenbury, Helen
Panek, Dennis
Peek, Merle
Prelutsky, Jack
Provensen, Alice and
Provensen, Martin
Rey, H. A.
Rockwell, Anne and
Rockwell, Harlow
Rylant, Cynthia
Selsam, Millicent E.
Sendak, Maurice
Sharmat, Marjorie Weinman
Steig, William
Steptoe, John
Szilagyi, Mary
Tejima
Ungerer, Tomi
Van Allsburg, Chris
Viorst, Judith
Waber, Bernard
Watson, Wendy
Wells, Rosemary
Wildsmith, Brian
Williams, Garth
Williams, Vera B.
Wood, Audrey and
Wood, Don
Zion, Eugene (Gene)
Zolotow, Charlotte

Appendix B
PICTURE BOOK CLASSICS

Books
for
Everychild
Picture
Book
Classics

A selection of 50 picture book classics, published since 1950, belonging in the literary life of every child's growing years.

Aardema, Verna. Why mosquitoes buzz in people's ears: a West African tale. Illus. by Leo Dillon and Diane Dillon. 1975. Dial. Ages 6-8.

Anno, Mitsumasa. Anno's counting book. Illus. by the author. 1977. Crowell. Ages 2-4.

Bang, Molly. Wiley and the Hairy Man: adapted from an American folk tale. Illus. by the author. 1976. Macmillan. Ages 6-8.

Baskin, Leonard and others. Hosie's alphabet. Illus. by Leonard Baskin. 1972. Viking. Ages 2-5.

Crews, Donald. Freight train. Illus. by the author. 1978. Greenwillow. Ages 2-5.

de Paola, Tomie. Strega Nona. Illus. by the author. 1975. Prentice-Hall. Ages 5-8.

de Regniers, Beatrice. May I bring a friend? Illus. by Beni Montresor. 1964. Atheneum. Ages 4-6.

Emberley, Barbara. Drummer Hoff. Illus. by Ed Emberley. 1967. Prentice-Hall. Ages 4-6.

Fatio, Louise. The happy lion. Illus. by Roger Duvoisin. 1964. McGraw-Hill. Ages 3-6.

Galdone, Paul. The three billy goats gruff. Retold and illus. by the author. 1973. Clarion. Ages 3-7.

Grimm, Jakob Ludwig Karl and Grimm, Wilhelm Karl. Snow White and the seven dwarfs. Retold by Randall Jarrell. Illus. by Nancy E. Burkert. 1972. Farrar. Ages 6-9.

Hill, Eric. Where's Spot? Illus. by the author. 1980. Putnam. Ages 3-5.

Hoban, Russell. Bedtime for Frances. Illus. by Garth Williams. 1960. Harper. Ages 4-6.

Hogrogian, Nonny. One fine day. Illus. by the author. 1971. Macmillan. Ages 5-7.

Hutchins, Pat. Rosie's walk. Illus. by the author. 1968. Macmillan. Ages 4-6.

Hyman, Trina Schart. Little Red Riding Hood. Retold and illus. by the author. 1983. Holiday. Ages 5-8.

Isadora, Rachel. Ben's trumpet. Illus. by the author. 1979. Greenwillow. Ages 6-8.

Keats, Ezra, J. The snowy day. Illus. by the author. 1962. Viking; Penguin/Puffin, paper. Ages. 4-6.

Kellogg, Steven. The island of the Skog. Illus. by the author. 1973. Dial. Ages 6-8.

Lionni, Leo. Alexander and the wind-up mouse. Illus. by the author. 1969. Pantheon. Ages 6-8.

Lobel, Arnold. Frog and Toad are friends. Illus. by the author. 1970. Harper. Ages 6-8.

London Bridge is falling down. Illus. by Peter Spier. 1967. Doubleday. Ages 3-5.

McDermott, Gerald. Arrow to the sun: A Pueblo Indian tale. Illus. by the author. 1974. Viking; Penguin/Puffin, paper. Ages 6-8.

Mahy, Margaret. The boy who was followed home. Illus. by Steven Kellogg. 1975. Dial/Pied Piper, paper. Ages 5-8.

Marshall, James. George and Martha. Illus. by the author. 1972. Houghton. Ages 5-7.

Mayer, Marianna. Beauty and the beast. Retold by the author. Illus. by Mercer Mayer. 1978. Four Winds Press. Ages 6-8.

Moeri, Louise. Star mother's youngest child. Illus. by Trina Schart Hyman. 1975. Houghton. Ages 6-8.

Moore, Clement C. The night before Christmas. Illus. by Tomie de Paola. 1980. Holiday. Ages 3-8.

Ness, Evaline. Sam, Bangs and Moonshine. Illus. by the author. 1966. Holt. Ages 6-8.

Oxenbury, Helen. Dressing; Family; Friends; Playing; Working. Illus. by the author. 1981. Simon & Schuster/ Little Simon. Ages 1-3.

Peet, Bill. Big Bad Bruce. Illus. by the author. 1971. Houghton. Ages 6-9.

Rayner, Mary. Mr. and Mrs. Pig's evening out. Illus. by the author. 1976. Atheneum. Ages 5-7.

Rice, Eve. Sam who never forgets. Illus. by the author. 1977. Greenwillow; Penguin/Puffin, paper. Ages 2-5.

Sendak, Maurice. Where the wild things are. Illus. by the author. 1963. Harper. Ages 5-8.

Seuss, Dr. Horton hears a Who. Illus. by the author. 1954. Random. Ages 3-5.

Shulevitz, Uri. One Monday morning. Illus. by the author. 1967. Scribner. Ages 5-7.

Steig, William. Sylvester and the magic pebble. Illus. by the author. 1969. Simon & Schuster/Windmill. Ages 6-8.

Steptoe, John. Stevie. Illus. by the author. 1969. Harper. Ages 6-8.

Stevenson, James. Could be worse! Illus. by the author. 1977. Greenwillow; Penguin/Puffin, paper. Ages 6-8.

Stevenson, Robert Louis. A child's garden of verses. Illus. by Tasha Tudor. 1981. Rand McNally. Ages 5-8.

Tripp, Wallace. A great big ugly man came up and tied his horse to me: a book of nonsense verse. Illus. by the author. 1973. Little, Brown. Ages 5-8.

Turkle, Brinton. Deep in the forest. Illus. by the author. 1976. Dutton. Ages 3-6.

Van Allsburg, Chris. Jumanji. Illus. by the author. 1981. Houghton. Ages 6-9.

Viorst, Judith. Alexander and the terrible, horrible, no good very bad day. Illus. by Ray Cruz. 1972. Atheneum. Ages 6-9.

Ward, Lynd. The biggest bear. Illus. by the author. 1953. Houghton. Ages 6-8.

Wells, Rosemary. Benjamin & Tulip. Illus. by the author. 1973. Dial. Ages 5-7.

Wildsmith, Brian. Brian Wildsmith's ABC. Illus. by the author. 1963. Watts. Ages 1-3.

Winter, Paula. The bear & the fly. Illus. by the author. 1976. Crown; Scholastic, paper. Ages 4-7.

Yashima, Taro. Crow boy. Illus. by the author. 1955. Viking; Penguin/Puffin, paper. Ages 5-7.

Zemach, Harve. Duffy and the devil. Illus. by Margot Zemach. 1973. Farrar. Ages 6-8.

PICTURE BOOKS THAT CELEBRATE CULTURAL DIVERSITY AND THE UNIVERSALITY OF HUMAN EXPERIENCE

Asian-American children

Bang, M. (1985). *The paper crane*. New York: Greenwillow.
Friedman, I. (1984). *How my parents learned to eat*. Boston: Houghton Mifflin.
Lee, J. M. (1985). *Toad is the uncle of heaven: A Vietnamese folk tale*. New York: Holt, Rinehart & Winston.
Louie, A. L. (1982). *Yeh Shen: A Cinderella story from China*. New York: Philomel.

Black children

Brenner, B. (1978). *Wagon wheels*. New York: Harper & Row.
Caines, J. (1982). *Just us women*. New York: Harper/Trophy.
Cameron, A. (1986). *More stories Julian tells*. New York: Knopf.
Daly, N. (1986). *Not so fast, Songololo*. New York: McElderry/Macmillan.
Flournoy, V. (1985). *The patchwork quilt*. New York: Dial.
Greenfield, E. (1978). *Honey, I love*. New York: Crowell.
Grifalconi, A. (1986). *The village of round and square houses*. New York: Macmillan/Four Winds.
Jonas, A. (1984). *Holes and peeks*. New York: Greenwillow.
Keats, E. J. (1975). *Louie*. New York: Scholastic.
Keats, E. J. (1962). *The snowy day*. New York: Viking.
Langstaff, J., Ed. (1987). *What a morning! The Christmas story in Black spirituals*. New York: Macmillian/McElderry.

Hispanic children

Alexander, F. (1981). *Mother Goose on the Rio Grande*. (Spanish for Young Americans series). Lincolnwood, IL: National Textbook.
Alonso, F. (1975). *La gallina Paulina y el grano de trigo: Cuento popular espanol* (Pauline the hen and the grain of wheat: Traditional story from Spain). Santillana, Spain: Follett.
Behrens, J. (1978). *Fiesta!* Chicago: Childrens Press.

Garcia, R. (1986). *My Aunt Otilia's spirits/Los espiritus de mi tia Otilia*. San Francisco: Children's Book Press.

Griego, M. C. (1980). *Tortillitas para mama*. New York: Holt, Rinehart & Winston.

Kouzel, D. (1977). *The cuckoo's reward/El premio del cuco*. New York: Doubleday.

Pomerantz, C. (1980). *The tamarindo puppy and other poems*. New York: Morrow.

Williams, V. B. (1982). *A chair for my mother*. New York: Greenwillow.

Native American children

Baker, O. (1981). *Where the buffaloes begin*. New York: Murray.

de Paola, T. (1983). *The legend of bluebonnet*. New York: Putnam.

Goble, P. (1980). *The gift of the sacred dog*. New York: Bradbury.

Martin, B., & Archambault, J. (1987). *Knots on a counting rope*. New York: Henry Holt.

Family diversity

Bauer, C. F. (1981). *My mom travels a lot*. New York: Puffin.

Blaine, M. (1975). *The terrible thing that happened at our house*. New York: Scholastic.

Brown, L. K., & Brown, M. (1986). *Dinosaurs divorce: A guide for changing families*. Boston: Little, Brown.

Gerstein, M. (1984). *The room*. New York: Harper & Row.

Hughes, S. (1977). *David and dog*. Englewood Cliffs, NJ: Prentice-Hall.

Peterson, J. W. (1977). *I have a sister. My sister is deaf*. New York: Harper & Row.

Rosenburg, M. (1984). *Being adopted*. New York: Lothrop, Lee & Shepard.

Vigna, J. (1981). *Daddy's new baby*. Niles, IL: Whitman.

Williams, V. B. (1981). *Three days on a river in a red canoe*. New York: Greenwillow.

Zolotow, C. (1974). *My grandson Lew*. New York: Harper/Trophy.

A SELECTED BIBLIOGRAPHY OF PICTURE BOOKS ON VIDEOCASSETTE

After children have learned to love a book, a videotaped version of the story can be a way of enjoying the story over and over again. Quality videocassettes such as the ones listed here are also a satisfying alternative to mediocre or poor television programming. Even children who seem disinterested in books can sometimes be lured into watching a videocassette. Then, after the child is captivated by the story, scrutinizing the book at her or his own pace can be a welcome opportunity.

Children's videocassettes should be selected with the same care as children's literature. Use these criteria to make choices.

- The subject matter must be particularly suitable for the video format.
- The program must be presented in an accurate, understandable, and pleasing manner.
- The overall level of technical production should approach broadcast quality.
- The program should encourage people to view the videocassette again and again.

Videocassette Title	Producer	Year Released on Video
Arthur's Eyes by Marc Brown	Children's Video Library	1987
Beauty and the Beast by Martha Hamilton & Mitch Weiss	Kartes Video	1981
Changes, Changes by Pat Hutchins	Weston Woods	1972
Charlie Needs a Cloak by Tomie de Paola	Weston Woods	1977
Curious George Rides a Bike by H. A. Rey	Weston Woods	1958
Digging Up Dinosaurs by Aliki	Children's Video Library	1981
Doctor De Soto (and other stories) by William Steig	Weston Woods	1985
The Cat in the Hat/Doctor Seuss on the Loose by Dr. Seuss	Playhouse Video	1974
The Emperor and the Nightingale by Hans Christian Andersen	Sony Video	1987

Videocassette Title	Producer	Year Released on Video
Five Lionni Classics by Leo Lionni	Random House	1985
The Foolish Frog by Pete and Charles Seeger	Weston Woods	1973
Harold and the Purple Crayon by Crockett Johnson	Weston Woods	1969
King Cole's Party (nursery rhymes) by the Wee Sing Players	Price/Stern/Sloan	1987
Little Prince and Friends	Pacific Arts Video	1987
Make Way for Ducklings by Robert McCloskey	Weston Woods	1955
Morris's Disappearing Bag by Rosemary Wells	Weston Woods	1984
The Snowman by Raymond Briggs	Sony	1982
The Tale of Mr. Jeremy Fisher and the Tale of Mr. Peter Rabbit by Beatrix Potter	Sony	1987
The Red Balloon by Albert Lamourise	Cable Films	1986
The Snowy Day by Ezra Jack Keats	Weston Woods	1964
Strega Nona Tomie de Paola	Weston Woods	1978
The Three Little Pigs *Tikki Tikki Tembo* retold by Arlene Mosel	CBS/Fox Video	1985
The Wind in the Willows by Kenneth Graham	Thorne/EMI	1984
Ugly Duckling by Hans Christian Andersen	Rabbit Ears Production	1986

For Further Information

Schechter, H. (1986). *Kidvid: A parents' guide to children's videos.* New York: Pocket Books.

Scholtz, J. C. (1988, February 1). Home video for libraries. *Booklist,* p. 944.

Jalongo, M. R. (1987). Children's videocassettes: How to choose them, ways to use them. *PTA Today, 12,* 16–18.

See also *Booklist* and *Parents' Choice,* two magazines that review children's media. Write: *Booklist,* American Library Association, 50 E. Huron St., Chicago, IL 60611 and *Parents' Choice,* Parents' Choice Foundation, Box 185, Newton, MA 02168.

INFORMATION ABOUT NAEYC

NAEYC is . . .

an organization of more than 103,000 members founded in 1926 and committed to fostering the growth and development of children from birth through age 8. Membership is open to all who share a desire to serve and act on behalf of the needs and rights of young children.

NAEYC provides . . .

educational services and resources to adults and programs working with and for children, including

• *Young Children,* the peer-reviewed journal for early childhood educators

• **Books, posters, brochures, and videos** to expand your knowledge and commitment to and support your work with young children and families, including topics on infants, curriculum, research, discipline, teacher education, and parent involvement

• **An Annual Conference** that brings people together from all over the United States and other countries to share their expertise and advocate on behalf of children and families

• **Week of the Young Child** celebrations sponsored by more than 400 NAEYC Affiliate Groups to call public attention to the critical significance of the child's early years

• **Insurance plans** for members and programs

• **Public affairs** information and access to information through NAEYC resources and communication systems for conducting knowledgeable advocacy efforts at all levels of government and through the media

• **A voluntary accreditation system** for high-quality programs for children through the National Academy of Early Childhood Programs

• **Resources and services** through the National Institute for Early Childhood Professional Development, working to improve the quality and consistency of early childhood preparation and professional development opportunities

• **Young Children International** to promote international communication and information exchanges

For information about membership, publications, or other NAEYC services, visit the NAEYC Website at **http://www.naeyc.org**

National Association for the Education of Young Children
1509 16th Street, NW, Washington, DC 20036-1426
202-232-8777 or 800-424-2460